Liberalism's Religion

How should liberalism understand – and deal with – religion? Cécile Laborde offers powerful new answers in her book *Liberalism's Religion*; this collection subjects that theory to critical scrutiny from an array of scholars, thereby advancing the scholarly debate.

Religion has recently become the object of a significant and growing literature in legal and political philosophy, addressing such fundamental questions as: What does it mean to guarantee religious freedom? When the religious freedom of some citizens appears in conflict with the religious freedom of others, what should be done? May religious reasons be legitimately invoked to justify political decisions, or should they be excluded from public deliberation? In the recent literature, the dominant liberal response to these questions is based on an egalitarian theory of religion.

In her major new work, *Liberalism's Religion*, Cécile Laborde argues that the prevailing liberal-egalitarian approach toward religion is misguided and in need of crucial revision. In doing so, she offers original answers to the fundamental questions in this debate, organised by her distinctive thesis that liberals must radically rethink how we conceive religion itself. This volume subjects her powerful new theory to scrutiny from an array of scholars, engaging each dimension of it. The volume includes a comprehensive reply by Laborde to the various points raised by these scholars, and therefore moves the debate forward, highlighting key issues that should be addressed in future work on religion and political philosophy.

This book was originally published as a special issue of the journal *Critical Review of International Social and Political Philosophy*.

Aurélia Bardon is Junior Professor in Political Theory at the University of Konstanz, Germany. Her research focuses on public justification, religion, secularism, and liberal neutrality.

Jeffrey W. Howard is Associate Professor of Political Theory at University College London, UK. He writes on free speech, criminal punishment, and democratic theory.

Liberalism's Religion
Cécile Laborde and Her Critics

Edited by
Aurélia Bardon and Jeffrey W. Howard

Routledge
Taylor & Francis Group

LONDON AND NEW YORK

First published 2020
by Routledge
2 Park Square, Milton Park, Abingdon, Oxon, OX14 4RN

and by Routledge
52 Vanderbilt Avenue, New York, NY 10017

Routledge is an imprint of the Taylor & Francis Group, an informa business

© 2020 Taylor & Francis

All rights reserved. No part of this book may be reprinted or reproduced or utilised in any form or by any electronic, mechanical, or other means, now known or hereafter invented, including photocopying and recording, or in any information storage or retrieval system, without permission in writing from the publishers.

Trademark notice: Product or corporate names may be trademarks or registered trademarks, and are used only for identification and explanation without intent to infringe.

British Library Cataloguing-in-Publication Data
A catalogue record for this book is available from the British Library

ISBN13: 978-0-367-50267-6

Typeset in Myriad Pro
by codeMantra

Publisher's Note
The publisher accepts responsibility for any inconsistencies that may have arisen during the conversion of this book from journal articles to book chapters, namely the inclusion of journal terminology.

Disclaimer
Every effort has been made to contact copyright holders for their permission to reprint material in this book. The publishers would be grateful to hear from any copyright holder who is not here acknowledged and will undertake to rectify any errors or omissions in future editions of this book.

Contents

Citation Information vi
Notes on Contributors viii

Introduction: Laborde, liberalism, and religion 1
Aurélia Bardon and Jeffrey W. Howard

1 Laborde's religion 9
  Sune Lægaard

2 Is epistemic accessibility enough? Same-sex marriage, tradition, and the Bible 21
  Aurélia Bardon

3 Defending broad neutrality 36
  Jeffrey W. Howard

4 On *Liberalism's Religion* 48
  Jean L. Cohen

5 Liberalism and religion: the plural grounds of separation 68
  Chiara Cordelli

6 The integrity of religious believers 81
  Paul Bou-Habib

7 Individual integrity, freedom of association and religious exemption 94
  Peter Jones

8 Religion and discrimination: extending the 'disaggregative approach' 109
  Daniel Sabbagh

9 Three cheers for liberal modesty 119
  Cécile Laborde

Index 137

Citation Information

The chapters in this book were originally published in the *Critical Review of International Social and Political Philosophy*, volume 23, issue 1 (Jan 2020). When citing this material, please use the original page numbering for each article, as follows:

Introduction
Laborde, liberalism, and religion
Aurélia Bardon and Jeffrey W. Howard
Critical Review of International Social and Political Philosophy, volume 23, issue 1 (Jan 2020) pp. 1–8

Chapter 1
Laborde's religion
Sune Lægaard
Critical Review of International Social and Political Philosophy, volume 23, issue 1 (Jan 2020) pp. 9–20

Chapter 2
Is epistemic accessibility enough? Same-sex marriage, tradition, and the Bible
Aurélia Bardon
Critical Review of International Social and Political Philosophy, volume 23, issue 1 (Jan 2020) pp. 21–35

Chapter 3
Defending broad neutrality
Jeffrey W. Howard
Critical Review of International Social and Political Philosophy, volume 23, issue 1 (Jan 2020) pp. 36–47

Chapter 4
On Liberalism's Religion
Jean L. Cohen
Critical Review of International Social and Political Philosophy, volume 23, issue 1 (Jan 2020) pp. 48–67

Chapter 5
Liberalism and religion: the plural grounds of separation
Chiara Cordelli
Critical Review of International Social and Political Philosophy, volume 23, issue 1 (Jan 2020) pp. 68–80

Chapter 6
The integrity of religious believers
Paul Bou-Habib
Critical Review of International Social and Political Philosophy, volume 23, issue 1 (Jan 2020) pp. 81–93

Chapter 7
Individual integrity, freedom of association and religious exemption
Peter Jones
Critical Review of International Social and Political Philosophy, volume 23, issue 1 (Jan 2020) pp. 94–108

Chapter 8
Religion and discrimination: extending the 'disaggregative approach'
Daniel Sabbagh
Critical Review of International Social and Political Philosophy, volume 23, issue 1 (Jan 2020) pp. 109–118

Chapter 9
Three cheers for liberal modesty
Cécile Laborde
Critical Review of International Social and Political Philosophy, volume 23, issue 1 (Jan 2020) pp. 119–135

For any permission-related enquiries please visit:
http://www.tandfonline.com/page/help/permissions

Contributors

Aurélia Bardon, Department of Politics and Public Administration, University of Konstanz, Germany.

Paul Bou-Habib, Department of Government, University of Essex, UK.

Jean L. Cohen, Department of Political Science, Columbia University, USA.

Chiara Cordelli, Department of Political Science, University of Chicago, USA.

Jeffrey W. Howard, Department of Political Science, University College London, UK.

Peter Jones, School of Geography, Politics and Sociology, Newcastle University, Newcastle upon Tyne, UK.

Cécile Laborde, Nuffield College, University of Oxford, UK.

Sune Lægaard, Department of Communication and Arts, Roskilde University, Denmark.

Daniel Sabbagh, Sciences Po, Centre de Recherches Internationales (CERI), Paris, France.

INTRODUCTION

Laborde, liberalism, and religion

Aurélia Bardon and Jeffrey W. Howard

ABSTRACT
In this introduction, we provide a brief overview of the debate on religion in political philosophy. We present the main arguments defended by Cécile Laborde in *Liberalism's Religion* and explain how these arguments contribute to the debate.

The state of the debate

Liberal states, in order to be truly liberal, must protect religious freedom. This means not only that citizens should be free to hold whatever religious beliefs they want, and to worship in whatever way they see fit, but also that they should be free to change religion whenever they want, or decide to have no religion at all. This commitment to religious freedom, including freedom from religion, is one of the few things that liberal political philosophers agree on. But, when it comes to religion, this might be the only thing that liberal political philosophers agree on.

Religion has recently become the object of a significant and growing literature in legal and political philosophy: What does it mean to guarantee religious freedom? When the religious freedom of some citizens appears in conflict with the religious freedom of others, what should be done? When the religious convictions of some individuals clash with generally applicable laws, should the state grant exemptions? Does freedom of religion require some kind of separation between church and state, or are religious freedom and religious establishment wholly compatible? What, if anything, should be the role of religion in the public life of a liberal society? May religious reasons be legitimately invoked to justify political decisions, or should they be excluded from public deliberation? Two main debates have emerged that organize this surfeit of questions. One focuses on the question of religious freedom, and in particular on whether religious commitments and practices merit special protection under law in virtue of their religious character. The other focuses on the question of separation and secularism, and in particular on whether religious commitments and practices should be contained by law, also in virtue of their religious character.

In the recent literature, the dominant liberal response to these questions is based on an egalitarian theory of religion, according to which 'religion need not be singled out in the liberal state' (Laborde, 2017, p. 13; see also, 2014). The roots of the liberal egalitarian view on religion can be found in the work of John Rawls (1971; 1993), as well as Ronald Dworkin (2013), Eisgruber and Sager (2007), and Maclure and Taylor (2011). The core claim of this egalitarian view is that religion, for legal and political purposes, is not special.[1] To the extent that religion should be protected by the state, it is because it is the subcategory of something larger that deserves protection. To the extent that religion should not be recognized or endorsed by a state, that it should be kept at a certain distance, or perhaps that it should be excluded from the public sphere, it is also because it is the subcategory of something larger that should be the object of state neutrality. On this view, religion should not be singled out for special treatment because it should be treated in exactly the same way as similar non-religious commitments are: the state should protect equally religious and non-religious conceptions of the good; it should be neutral toward religion because it should be more generally neutral toward the good; it should not promote any particular religion, and it should not promote religion over non-religion, because the liberal state should not promote any particular controversial comprehensive doctrine; and it should eschew sectarian religious arguments in public justification simply because it should eschew sectarian arguments generally.

What, exactly, is religion supposedly a subcategory of? If religion *qua* religion is not a relevant category for the liberal state, what is the relevant category that religion belongs to? How is this relevant category defined, identified, and delimited? Egalitarian theorists identify this larger relevant category as that of 'the good' or 'conceptions of the good'. Liberal egalitarianism is then better understood through its fundamental commitment to neutrality toward *that*. There are two ways in which the egalitarian state is neutral in contrast to a state that would single out religion for special treatment. First, singling out religion would require a justification: what makes religion a special kind of good? What is especially valuable about religion? Identifying some intrinsic religious good would explain why religion should be protected in a way that no non-religious commitment should be protected, because religion is intrinsically different from non-religious activities (Laycock, 1990, p. 16, McConnell, 1985, p. 18). However, any attempt to justify the special good of religion would be fundamentally non-neutral: the liberal state cannot neutrally maintain that religion in itself matters and is, more than anything else, protection-worthy. Because egalitarian theorists deny that religion should be singled out, they successfully avoid this problem: they do not have to justify why religion is uniquely valuable. Second, singling out of religion would require a particular definition of religion: what counts as religious, and therefore what kinds of practices or commitments should be singled out for special treatment? Distinguishing between what is religious and what is not religious is only possible based on some particular conception of religion, but any particular conception of religion will be necessarily controversial and non-neutral (Sullivan, 2007). This second issue is also avoided by egalitarian theorists: since religion is not singled out for special treatment, the distinction between religious and non-religious commitments or practices is not relevant, and therefore no particular definition of religion is needed.

Liberal egalitarianism, then, does not require either a justification of the protection-worthiness of religion, or a particular definition of religion. It can refrain from answering both challenges. Or so, anyway, it would seem.

Reconceiving the debate

In her major new work, *Liberalism's Religion*, Cécile Laborde argues that the prevailing liberal-egalitarian approach toward religion is misguided and in need of crucial revision. It is false, she believes, that egalitarianism can avoid the twin aforementioned challenges; it only displaces them, forcing them to reappear at a more fundamental level in the theory. The first main section of the book, Chapters 1–3, establishes this argument through exhaustive critical engagement with the existing scholarly literature. First, Laborde argues that egalitarianism faces what she terms *the problem of ethical salience*. Even if the category of protection-worthy commitments is not limited to religious ones – thereby alleviating the need to explain why religion in particular is protection-worthy – egalitarians still need to explain why the general category in question is protection-worthy. '[L]iberalism, for all its claims to neutrality', she writes, 'cannot dispense with an ethical evaluation of the salience of different conceptions, beliefs, and commitments' (p. 5).[2] Without such an ethical evaluation, one cannot explain why, for instance, conscientious commitments are more valuable than mere preferences, and why exemptions might be required to accommodate the former but not the latter.

Second, egalitarians insist that they can avoid the question of what qualifies as 'religious', but they cannot avoid a deeper question, what Laborde terms *the jurisdictional boundary problem*. This problem concerns the way in which the liberal sovereign state distinguishes between public and private – what is the focus of the state's legitimate business, and what falls outside it. Laborde contends that there is no non-neutral way for the state to identify the boundaries of what belongs to the private sphere, and of what falls under the scope of political authority: 'even assuming that liberals can justify that the state should concern itself with interpersonal justice, they need to justify the state's prerogative to set the boundaries of where interpersonal justice lies in the first place, in the context of foundational disagreement about the boundary of justice itself' (p. 107). In other words, the commitment to neutrality challenge is far more difficult to maintain than egalitarian theorists have usually assumed.

By demonstrating how these two problems afflict existing liberal-egalitarian views, the first three chapters of *Liberalism's Religion* reveal that the common analogy between *religion* and *the good* is seriously problematic. That is why, Laborde argues, this analogy should be replaced by what she terms a *disaggregative approach*. There is not one single value in religion; there is a plurality of values, and none of them can be uniquely associated with religion. Religion is sometimes a conception of the good, but it can also be many other things, including a conscientious obligation, a feature of identity, a mode of human association, a vulnerability class, a totalizing institution, or an inaccessible doctrine (Laborde, 2015, pp. 594–595).

The second main part of this book directly applies Laborde's original framework to the pressing questions about religion in contemporary political and legal philosophy. Harnessing her disaggregative approach, Laborde identifies the connection between secularism and liberalism (Chapter 4), and she responds to the jurisdictional boundary problem (Chapter 5) and to the ethical salience problem (Chapter 6).

In Chapter 4, Laborde argues that the liberal state has to be a minimally secular state, which means it has to be a *justifiable* state, an *inclusive* state, and a *limited* state. Each of these three components of secularism singles out a particular dimension of religion, but none of them exclusively concerns religion. First, the justifiable state is a state that provides public justification for coercive state action. What it singles out is the non-accessible dimension of religion. But non-religious reasons can be non-accessible in exactly the same way as religious reasons can be non-accessible. Non-accessible reasons, whether they are religious are not, are impermissible sources of public justification (pp. 117–132). Second, the inclusive state is a state that treats all of its citizens as equals. What it singles out is the divisive dimension of religion. But non-religious identities can be just as divisive as religious ones. The inclusive state requires that civic identity is not associated with any divisive feature of identity, whether it is religious or not (pp. 132–143). Finally, the limited state is a state that respects the sovereignty of individuals over their private sphere. What it singles out is the comprehensive dimension of religion. But comprehensive doctrines need not be religious. In a limited state, comprehensive conceptions of the good should not be enforced on individuals, whether they are religious or not (pp. 143–150). None of the three dimensions of secularism, then, uniquely concerns religion. The defense of minimal secularism, in other words, is fundamentally egalitarian. Whenever it is justified or required to have a separation between religion and politics, it applies equally to those reasons, identities, and conceptions of the good that have the same features of non-accessibility, divisiveness, and comprehensiveness.

In Chapter 5, Laborde confronts the jurisdictional boundary problem. She shows that controversies about the proper scope of religious autonomy are themselves political controversies that must be resolved by the state. In this way, the state does not and must not share final decision-making sovereignty with non-state institutions; 'the authoritative and stable resolution of conflicts about justice' – including conflicts about the scope of religious freedom and the legitimate prerogatives of religious associations – 'requires a final, ultimate source of sovereignty' (p. 161). This, Laborde insists, is a central component of secularism, which 'locates the source of [state] sovereignty in a social contract' (p. 163). Those who insist that God has sovereignty over a particular domain, and that the liberal state must be constricted accordingly, must be opposed – a difficult position for egalitarians who mistakenly believe they can remain neutral on such questions. Notwithstanding this defense of state sovereignty, Laborde argues that such sovereignty must be exercised in accordance with liberal principles, which she believes demand broad rights to free association – for religious and non-religious groups alike. This sometimes justifies religious groups' exemption from generally applicable legislation, such as concerning non-discrimination. To be entitled to exemptions, Laborde argues that associations must be *voluntary* (i.e. exit is not unreasonably costly) and *identificatory* (i.e. individuals join the groups to pursue their conception of the good) (pp. 173–174). She also holds that such groups must pass a test of *coherence*, such that they have the 'ability to live by their own standards, purposes and commitments' (p. 175), and a test of *competence*, such that they possess expertise in how to 'interpret their own standards, purposes, and commitments' (p. 175). Laborde demonstrates how this framework is superior to the prevailing 'ministerial exception' doctrine at explaining why, for example, the Catholic Church may enjoy a legal permission to hire only male clergy, and she applies the framework to a variety of pressing political and legal controversies about the proper scope of religious associational autonomy.

In Chapter 6, Laborde confronts the problem of ethical salience to determine the conditions under which individuals should be granted exemptions from generally applicable laws. Liberal egalitarians, she thinks, are mistaken to assume that they can avoid the ethical salience problem because they do not single out religion. If exemptions can be granted for conscientious claims or deep commitments, including religious ones, it has to be because such claims or commitments are considered as ethically salient. The state, Laborde argues, must make judgments about the comparative ethical salience of different interests. How else, she asks, is the state to decide which liberties are basic, or which rights are most important? Laborde develops a 'two-pronged test'; a candidate exemption claim must pass both to succeed. The first prong inquires into whether the practice embodies 'specific normative values that the law has reason to protect' (p. 202). This occurs, in Laborde's view, if the practice implicates participants' *integrity* – 'an ideal of congruence between one's ethical commitments and one's actions' (p. 203). When it does, commitment to engaging in the practice is an *identity-protecting commitment* (IPC). Integrity requires what Laborde terms *thick sincerity*; the citizen must genuinely believe that her ethical convictions demand the IPC in question. However, while integrity is necessary to pass the first stage, it is not sufficient. The IPC must also meet what Laborde terms *thin acceptability*; the practice in question must be compatible with the most minimal moral standards. If the commitment is morally abhorrent – as in the case of someone demanding an exemption from laws banning murder in order to practice infant sacrifice – it has no *pro tanto* moral value, and so is disqualified *ab initio*. But provided the IPC is at least morally ambivalent (p. 209), it passes the first stage and is considered at the second stage, which addresses the costs that the exemption would impose on others to determine whether it would be fair all-things-considered. At this stage, Laborde fruitfully distinguishes between *Obligation-IPCs* – which implicate citizens' conscience – and *Identity-IPCs* – which implicate their identity. She defends the moral imperative of protecting citizens' *obligation-IPCs* from disproportionate burdens that can be alleviated without excessive cost. And she defends the importance of protecting citizens' *identity-IPCs* from majority status quo bias, which makes it difficult for citizens from minority cultures and religions to pursue socially valuable opportunities while maintaining their identity (pp. 215–217).

The road ahead

The original contributions of Laborde's new treatise are manifold, and it would be impossible to summarize them all here. But two are especially worthy of noticing . First, central to Laborde's accomplishment is her insistence that liberal egalitarians cease to regard religion as a monolithic category that poses special problems for political theory. Instead we must disaggregate religion into its constituent elements, and thereby illuminate the various general categories to which these elements respectively belong – some of which require protection, others containment. Second, we must realize that the vexed controversies about the place of religion in a liberal society are not to be resolved by simply insisting that we can be neutral toward such controversies. Nor can they be resolved by insisting that our religious authorities command a dominion over us that the state must regard as outside its ambit of sovereign concern. The continuing battles over religion in public life are political controversies, admitting of intense but reasonable disagreements that can only be settled through respectful democratic deliberation and decision-making. We view this symposium, intended to subject Laborde's powerful new theory to analytic scrutiny, as a contribution to that deliberation.

Notes

1. It should be noted that one could distinguish between two different understandings of *special*. Egalitarians claim that religion should not be *singled out for special treatment*. However, some of them believe that religion, to the extent that it belongs to a category of particularly important commitments, *deserves special protection*. On the distinction between the two understandings, see Patten (2017, pp. 212–213) and Bardon and Ceva (forthcoming).
2. Unless otherwise indicated, page references are to Laborde (2017).

Acknowledgments

This special issue is based on a symposium on Cécile Laborde's manuscript *Liberalism's Religion* that took place at University College London in June 2016. Special thanks are due especially to Paul Billingham and Albert Weale, whose critical feedback was indispensable.

Disclosure statement

No potential conflict of interest was reported by the authors.

Funding

This study was funded by the [ERC Grant 283867] on 'Is Religion Special?

References

Bardon, A., & Ceva, E. (forthcoming). The ethics of toleration and religious accommodations. In A. Lever & A. Poama (eds), *The routledge handbook of ethics and public policy*. London: Rouledge.

Dworkin, R. (2013). *Religion without god*. Cambridge, MA: Harvard University Press.

Eisgruber, C., & Sager, L. (2007). *Religious freedom and the constitution*. Cambridge, MA: Harvard University Press.

Laborde, C. (2014). Equal liberty, non-establishment and religious freedom. *Legal Theory*, *20*(1), 52–77.

Laborde, C. (2015). Religion in the law: The disaggregative approach. *Law and Philosophy*, *34*, 581–600.

Laborde, C. (2017). *Liberalism's religion*. Cambridge, MA: Harvard University Press.

Laycock, D. (1990). The remnants of free exercise. *The Supreme Court Review*, *1990*, 1–68.

Maclure, J., & Taylor, C. (2011). *Secularism and freedom of conscience*. Cambridge, MA: Harvard University Press.

McConnell, M. (1985). Accommodation of religion. *The Supreme Court Review*, *1985*, 1–59.

Patten, A. (2017). Religious exemptions and fairness. In C. Laborde & A. Bardon (eds.), *Religion in Liberal political philosophy* (pp. 204–219). Oxford: Oxford University Press.

Rawls, J. (1971). *A theory a justice*. Cambridge, Massachusetts: Belknap Press of Harvard University Press.

Rawls, J. (1993). *Political Liberalism*. New York, NY: Columbia University Press.

Sullivan, W. F. (2007). *The impossibility of religious freedom*. Princeton, NJ: Princeton University Press.

Laborde's religion

Sune Lægaard

ABSTRACT
Cécile Laborde's *Liberalism's Religion* proposes liberal principles to address political controversies over religion. One is the public reason requirement that reasons for state policies should be accessible. Another is the civic inclusiveness requirement according to which symbolic religious establishment is wrong when it communicates that religious identity is a component of civic identity. A third is the claim that liberal states have meta-jurisdictional authority to settle the boundary between what counts as religion and what counts as non-religion. The article considers whether Laborde has managed to articulate these three principles in a way that is operationalisable and can serve to provide solutions to practical controversies over religion. It is argued that Laborde's formulations leave important issues open, and some ways of settling these issues are considered.

In *Liberalism's Religion*, Cécile Laborde aims 'to provide reasoned solutions' to political controversies over religion (Laborde, 2017, p. 4). At the same time, she aims to provide a diagnosis of the way liberal political philosophy has understood and treated religion. She mainly aims to do the former by way of doing the latter. Her proposed solutions to particular political controversies over religion are accordingly specifically *liberal* solutions. The principles she proposes as providing these solutions are furthermore articulated by way of an examination of how liberal political philosophers have recently struggled with religion.

This is both a much-needed and a sensible approach. Liberals are more torn about religion than proponents of many other political views, for example, conservatives and socialists. There has furthermore long been a tendency for insufficiently worked out liberal ideas, such as notions about neutrality, separation, and rights, to spill over in to public political debates about religion in ways that have often not contributed to real 'solutions' but have rather tended to exacerbate existing conflicts.

This means that Laborde's solutions are actually more about liberalism than about religion, more about what should *matter* to liberalism than what religion *is* in some deeper sense. This is not a problem but arguably a strength of Laborde's approach – as long as one keeps it in mind.

So one can ask two kinds of questions to Laborde's book. One concerns her diagnosis of how liberalism should understand and handle religion. Is her disaggregation approach on the right track? Is her interpretation of the liberal philosophers of religion on which she bases her own theory reasonable? Does she succeed in identifying the right dimensions of religion that should actually matter from a liberal perspective, or are some missing?

The other kind of question one might ask concerns the solutions to political controversies over religion that Laborde proposes on this basis. The relevant question here is not whether she interprets Dworkin, Quong, or Eisgruber and Sager correctly or whether she manages to provide an exhaustive picture of what a liberal theory of religion should include. The question then rather concerns whether the principles she proposes for handling specific kinds of controversies can actually do the job. Can they be applied in a way yielding the promised solutions? And are the policy prescriptions that follow from them plausible?

In my comments, I will ask the latter kind of question. My discussion will – as it were – concern the output side of Laborde's book rather than the input side, that is, the second part of the book rather than the first part. This is not because I find the input side less relevant – in fact, I very much agree with Laborde's overall disaggregation approach. I have very little to quarrel with here. But what makes an extensive discussion of 'Liberalism's religion' worthwhile and important is not exegetical discussions of how to understand specific philosophers but rather that religious controversies are very salient in contemporary politics and an important motivation for liberal political philosophy. So let us concentrate on whether Laborde's take on liberalism's religion can actually help us in providing reasoned solutions to controversies that motivate us in the first place.

To consider this, I will pick out a few of the central outputs of Laborde's theory. I will mainly ask whether the proposed principles can do the job of providing solutions. I ask this, not in the hope of revealing reasons for rejecting Laborde's theory, since I agree with the overall approach. I rather ask this in order to focus on her practical contribution and where it might need to be further developed.

The accessibility condition

The first respect in which religion can be problematic from the point of view of liberalism that Laborde identifies concerns an *epistemic* wrong:

> when the state appeals to the authority of a particular God, non-adherents are coerced in the name of reasons that they do not understand and cannot engage with: they are not respected as *democratic reasoners*. (p. 112)

This is the well-known topic of debates about public reason, namely religion used in the *justification* of state policies. Laborde proposes that it is a necessary, not a sufficient, condition for the liberal legitimacy of policies that reasons are accessible:

> The basic thought is that state-proffered *reasons* for laws must be articulated in a language that members of the public can understand and engage with. There are epistemic constraints on the *inputs* into public debate – what I call constraints of public reason *stricto sensu*. Official justification by the state should not appeal to reasons that actual citizens find inaccessible: that they cannot understand and discuss as reasons. (p. 113)

On this basis, Laborde articulates what she labels 'Principle 1 of minimal liberal secularism':

> *when a reason is not generally accessible, it should not be appealed to by state officials to justify state coercion.* (pp. 113–114)

Laborde distinguishes the accessibility condition from two competing positions in debates about public reason. One is the inclusivist position championed by convergence theorists such as Gerald Gaus and Kevin Vallier, who advocate an *intelligibility condition* according to which reasons for laws should merely be understandable in relation to the specific doctrine or epistemic standards of the speaker. For inclusivists, a law can be in accordance with public reason if other citizens can understand how there are reasons for it relative to the beliefs of the legislator, whether or not citizens themselves share or are even in a position to evaluate these beliefs. Laborde finds that this is a too weak condition since it does not respect citizens who are coerced by laws as democratic reasoners: they cannot engage with reasons if they are not accessible.

On the other hand, Laborde distinguishes her view from exclusivist positions based on a more exacting *shareability condition* according to which reasons for laws have to be endorsed according to common standards. She notes that exclusivist views both tend to assume a too strong anti-perfectionism and that the public reason requirement has to do all the work of ensuring liberal legitimacy. Since she rejects both assumptions, accessibility seems enough as far as the public reason requirement goes – since citizens who are coerced by laws can understand and assess the reasons proposed for laws even if they cannot endorse them according to common standards.

The difference between the three positions seems to follow from the combination of two independent distinctions, which Laborde presents in the following diagram (p. 113):

	Agent's own standards	Common standards
Understanding	Intelligibility	Accessibility
Endorsement	X	Shareability

So Laborde's position is based on two claims, namely

(1) that *the relevant standard* against which to assess reasons proposed in justification of coercive laws are common standards, that is, that laws are not liberally legitimate if they are only justified with reference to the standards of the agent proposing the law
(2) that a law can be liberally legitimate even if citizens coerced by it cannot endorse the reasons for it, as long as they can understand and assess the reasons.

I agree with Laborde's defences against inclusivist/convergence positions based on an intelligibility condition and exclusivist positions based on a shareability condition. So my critical comment regarding the accessibility condition is not based on a normative preference for one of the competing positions. Rather, my remarks concern whether the accessibility condition is formulated in a way suited to do the job it is supposed to do.

My first question concerns the difference between endorsement and understanding required for the distinction between the accessibility condition and the shareability condition to hold up. We have to consider this in connection with the understanding of the other distinction between the 'agent's own standards' and 'common standards' since endorsement and understanding both have to be understood relative to the latter.

The reference to 'standards' is not very precise. It is not clear what counts as a 'standard' at all. One plausible way to understand this is in light of Jonathan Quong's definition of foundational disagreement, which Laborde discusses earlier. Disagreement is foundational when it goes 'all the way down' in the sense that we 'share no premise from which to disagree, no justificatory framework that would allow us to weigh the merits and flaws of one another's views' (p. 91). If we read the distinction between agent's own standards and shared standards in light of this idea, then the former denotes foundational disagreement, because parties have no shared premise, whereas the latter means that there is not foundational disagreement but that parties share some premise.

If we proceed form this understanding of the first distinction, however, then the question is how we should understand the difference between accessibility and shareability. Both are consensus positions in the sense that they require common standards. But if this in turn means that people have to have shared premises, it becomes hard to see how the distinction between accessibility and shareability can be sustained; if people share premises, isn't understanding a reason in relation to these shared premises tantamount to endorsing the reason? If I understand a reason in relation to a premise that I share, how can I not also endorse the reason? This threatens to collapse the room for epistemic positions between foundational disagreement (convergence positions) and actual substantive agreement (consensus positions).

How can we understand the accessibility/shareability distinction so that it does not collapse in this way? One possibility is to say that it turns on the argument *from* the shared premise *to* a given law. This would be a specification of what we should understand by 'reason' in public reason views, which is often not explained very well. In many such debates, 'reason' merely denotes any consideration that counts in favour of a law. However, neither empirical claims nor normative principles support laws when taken in isolation. The claims that 'tax law X will generate revenue Y' or 'tax law X conforms to distributional principle Z' do not count in favour of law X unless we also have an independent commitment to principle Z or to raising revenue Y for other reasons. We need to distinguish between 'reason' in the sense of a particular (empirical or normative) claim and 'reason' in the sense of an argument linking a number of claims to a law. In the first sense, 'reason' denotes a claim functioning as a premise in an argument, while in the latter sense, 'reason' denotes the argument as a whole.

On this understanding, shareability requires that parties endorse the entire argument from their shared premises to the law in question (in which case we can talk of shared justification). Public reason then requires *both* that people have common standards in the sense that they share premises *and* that they agree that these premises provide *pro tanto* justification for a given law. Accessibility, on the other hand, merely requires shared premises but allows that people disagree about the argument from the premises to the law in question (in which case we can talk about accessible justification). This would allow for the apparently common phenomenon that people can agree on the relevant normative premises (e.g. policy aims) and still disagree about whether a law is justified (i.e. policy means), for example, if they at the same time have different assessments about the empirical consequences of adopting the policy.

This way of understanding the distinction would preserve the difference between accessibility and shareability.

The next question is whether we can apply the accessibility condition in a way allowing us to separate accessible from inaccessible justifications, which is what is required for it to actually provide a solution to the problems of concern to public reason debates. In other words, how do we determine whether a given justification actually is accessible?

Laborde does not directly say anything about this other than the already-noted formulations about citizens being able to *understand* and *assess* reasons for laws according to common standards. Her main concern is to show that the accessibility condition is not unfairly biased against religion since it does not amount to picking out religious reasons as especially problematic. She rather stresses that accessibility is not the same as secularity. Reasons based on private personal experience can be just as inaccessible as religious revelations. On the other hand (contra positions such as that of Robert Audi), reasons can be accessible even if they are religious. Religious reasons need not depend on inaccessible premises. In those cases, religious reasons are not excluded by her preferred public reason requirement.

But how do we know? Laborde remarks that her view is an 'empirical theory of public reason' (p. 123). This first of all means that we cannot know beforehand whether religious reasons are accessible or not; this is a *contingent* question the answer to which depends on specific facts about the particular case. The theory therefore requires us to evaluate reasons case by case. While this provides Laborde with a plausible rejoinder to the inclusivist charge that public reason requirements unfairly single out religious reasons for exclusion, it simultaneously places a burden on her theory. We cannot *do* what the theory requires unless we have a *criterion* of accessibility against which we can conduct the case-by-case assessment of reasons.

This might place Laborde in a dilemma. She writes that 'public reasons are reasons that actual (not idealized) publics find accessible' (p. 114). This suggests that the required criterion is also empirical in the additional sense that it concerns whether *actual* members of the public *in fact* understand reasons. This would make for an in principle operationalisable criterion of accessibility (albeit one requiring potentially extensive empirical research). But this way of specifying the criterion would go against the tendency in most public reason theory, which has moved away from *actual* endorsement towards either counterfactual endorsement (under the relevant circumstances, an agent *would* accept the law) or *rationally required* endorsement (under the relevant circumstances, agents *should* accept the law) (Vallier & D'Agostino, 2014, sect. 2.1).

Why does Laborde nevertheless opt for a reading of the accessibility condition as relative to what actual citizens find accessible? Instead of discussing this issue, however, Laborde focuses on whether public reason should be a merely epistemic or a more demanding substantive requirement. Epistemic requirements concerns the conditions for knowing whether a claim holds, whereas substantive conditions concern the content of the claim. Liberalism as an epistemic position says, for example, that the reasons for laws should be accessible to citizens. Liberalism as a substantive position says that laws should, for example, respect individual liberty and treat people as equals. Laborde agrees with the latter but argues that the substantive conditions are separate from the public reason requirement, which is purely epistemic.

The epistemic/substantive distinction is not, however, the same as the distinction between whether or not epistemic requirements should be understood relative to actual citizens. Even if one accepts Laborde's distinction between public reason as purely epistemic and substantive liberal requirements on the content of laws, there is still the issue whether epistemic accessibility is a function of the *kind* of reasons or of *the agent's* competence and background knowledge. Although she qualifies her view slightly in a footnote (p. 114, fn. 293), Laborde's answer suggests an *agent-relative* rather than a *reason-relative* perspective: accessibility is matter of what actual citizens can understand rather than of the *kind* and *source* of the reasons. But the two distinctions cut across each other:

	Agent-relative	Reason-relative
Epistemic	The reasons for laws should be accessible to actual citizens (Laborde's view)	The reasons for laws should be of certain types, e.g. derive from certain types of sources.
Substantive	Legitimacy depends on whether specific people agree with the reason, irrespectively of what the reason is (not necessarily a liberal view)	The liberal permissibility of laws can be entirely derived from the liberal pedigree of the reasons that are brought to justify them (Laborde's reading of Quong's view, p. 116)

If one opts for hypothetical or rationally required endorsement, this tends towards a reason-relative perspective: if reasons of certain types are available for a law, then sufficiently informed citizens *would* or *should* endorse the law, not the other way round. If Laborde is right that public reason is distinct from substantive liberal values, then hypothetical endorsement might be grounded on epistemic features of reasons rather than on a requirement that they have a liberal content. But then one could side with Laborde on the epistemic/substantive issue and still disagree with her agent-relative reading of accessibility. Moreover, by doing so one would arguably be in respectable company, since this amounts to going for hypothetical rather than actual endorsement.

Additional argument is required to justify Laborde's agent-relative position. This justification has to answer the question why it is not sufficient to provide agents with *actually accessible* reasons whether or not they happen to *understand* (or agree with) them? If we take the agent-relative reading seriously, then the wrong of not respecting people as democratic reasoners threatens to expand to attach to a much broader range of policies as soon as they are based on any claim that any actual citizens might find hard to understand (e.g. fiscal policies based on advanced economic models or environmental laws based on climate science). Do we really want to exclude such policies as liberally illegitimate?

So in order for Laborde's theory to actually provide the promised kind of solution, it needs to be specified with respect to a specific criterion of accessibility. Moreover, once we start to do this, it runs in to difficult questions about applicability that revive classic issues about actual versus hypothetical consent and where Laborde has yet to provide a full defence of her preferred position.

The inclusiveness condition

I now move from the epistemic to the substantive part of Laborde's minimal secularism. While accessibility of reasons is necessary for liberal legitimacy, it is not sufficient. The first additional condition is that a liberal state also has to treat people as equals. Laborde discusses this requirement with respect to cases of symbolic establishment, that is, cases where the state officially endorses some religion but still respects the equal rights (to religious liberty and non-discrimination) of citizens who are not adherents of the established religion. Since states might do this for non-religious reasons, for example, for reasons of social cohesion, such cases need not breach epistemic requirements of public reason and do not infringe on individual liberty. So what is wrong with symbolic establishment?

> Symbolic religious establishment is wrong when it communicates that religious identity is a component of civic identity – of what it means to be a citizen of that state -, and thereby deny civic status to those who do not endorse that identity, who are then treated as second-class citizens. (p. 129)

Again, Laborde's main message is that it is not religion – here in the form of establishment – that matters; what matters is the liberal value of civic equality. Establishment is wrong if it makes religion a part of civic identity, but not if it does not do this.

In a way quite similar to how she presented her accessibility condition as an 'empirical theory of public reason', Laborde stresses that 'the criterion of civic inclusiveness is singularly context-dependent' (p. 132). This makes it a contingent question whether establishment is wrong, which has to be assessed on a case-by-case basis.

I agree with Laborde here. But just as in the case of the accessibility condition, the inclusiveness condition raises a similar follow up question: if we are not concerned with religion *as such*, but with civic equality, how do we then determine whether a given instance of establishment is acceptable or not? Laborde is most concerned with showing that she does not single religion out as special. But in doing so she does not say much about the criterion of civic inclusiveness that is supposed to replace it. Her concluding passage is characteristic of this:

> In sum, the wrongness of state-endorsed religious symbols should be assessed in relation to the following criteria. First, it is not religion-dependent: it does not hinge on the semantic meaning of religion but, rather, relies on an interpretation of its social meaning as one possible suspect category for purposes of social discrimination and domination. Second, it is not person-dependent: it does not hinge on individuals' perceptions of exclusion or domination; nor does it hinge on whether individuals positively associate with the group or identity that is excluded from state endorsement. Third, it is context-dependent: social meanings vary from society to society. Fourth, it is symbol-dependent: different symbols can have different social meanings in different locations. (p. 134)

As a statement supposed to sum up what makes state endorsement of religion wrong, this passage is plainly inadequate – the two first 'criteria' are almost purely negative in that they only say what the criterion of civic inclusiveness *is not*. The third and fourth 'criteria' – although formulated in more positive terms – boil down to the negative message that there is no general answer across contexts about when establishment is wrong. The only positive specification is that we should assess each case in terms of whether establishment violates civic equality. But how do we do this? To make these case-by-case assessments, we need – again – a *criterion* of civic inclusiveness, which *defines and picks out* the relevant kind of equality in particular cases. Laborde elsewhere suggests that civic inclusion has to do with non-domination and is a sort of social equality, but this still falls short of an applicable criterion.

So while Laborde succeeds in sketching the contours of a theory that does not pick out religion as special, she does not say much about the specific content of the criterion of civic equality that is supposed to do the job in this theory. Therefore, it cannot yet provide solutions to political controversies over establishment.

Meta-jurisdictional sovereignty

The standard figure of thought in debates about secularism is the idea of *separation*. Secularism is about separation of church and state and of politics and religion more generally. Laborde's book nuances and qualifies this idea – there is not one kind of separation, but many; they concern different aspects of religion, not religion *as such*, and these aspects are instances of several more general normative liberal concerns. These points nevertheless still leave us with a (nuanced and qualified) version of the idea of separation.

This means that there still will be cases where politics and religion, church and state, have to be separated. In real-life politics, this figure has led to the further idea that, in such cases, churches and the state are somehow equal authorities with sovereignty within their respective spheres of competence. This is the idea of *church autonomy*, which has found expression in a number of ways – from the classical standoff between the Catholic Church and European princes, to recent court cases where private businesses have claimed – and won – exemptions from anti-discrimination law and mandatory health insurance based on the freedom of religion of their owners.

Even if one accepts Laborde's disaggregation approach, one could still claim church autonomy and hold that states have no authority over religious associations, communities and businesses. On such a view, freedom of religion is not a right granted by the state but an expression of state sovereignty giving way to religious sovereignty – analogous to the territorial border between states where one jurisdiction stops and another begins.

In Chapter 5, Laborde identifies and discusses this issue as what she helpfully labels 'the Jurisdictional Boundary problem'. This is first of all a problem in the sense that there is an issue here that needs to be addressed – the boundary has to be drawn for any idea of separation or neutrality to work. However, it is furthermore a problem for the traditional articulation of liberalism in terms of neutrality, because this decision is not itself a neutral one.

It is a major contribution of Laborde's book to acknowledge this issue as one liberalism has to address. The traditional claim that liberalism is about neutrality has blinded liberals to exactly this issue and exposed them to warranted criticism. Furthermore, the same idea has in fact provided support for claims about church autonomy assumed by the noted kind of court decisions. The idea of liberalism as neutrality has thereby provided support for recent attacks on liberal anti-discrimination and health insurance laws.

In light of this, Laborde's even more important contribution is that she clearly bites the bullet and asserts that liberal egalitarians cannot avoid granting the state the 'meta-jurisdictional authority' to delimitate the proper boundaries of religion: Liberal democratic legitimacy presupposes the final authority of the state in solving the Jurisdictional Boundary question (p. 155). Liberalism cannot only be a theory of justice and separation; it also has to be a theory about the sovereign state:

> One of its rightful prerogatives is what constitutional theorists call *Kompetenz-Kompetenz*: it has the competence to decide the respective areas of competence of associations within it. To use my preferred terminology, the state has the competence to adjudicate Jurisdictional Boundary questions. (p. 156)

This theory of state sovereignty of course has to be a *liberal* theory, and so meta-jurisdictional authority is a function of liberal legitimacy:

> once a state enjoys liberal legitimacy, it has, in addition, the prerogative to fix the more determinate boundary between what counts as religion and what counts as non-religion, in more specific controversies about which there is reasonable disagreement about justice. (p. 157, fn. 387)

This idea has two elements. One is that the category of religion is not a natural category but is in fact constructed and constituted by the state. The state decides what counts as religion. Before the state installed this difference, religion was not distinct from other spheres. Therefore, it makes no sense when proponents of church autonomy appeal to a separate and pre-existing religious sovereignty, which is on a par with state sovereignty, because religion is a product of the state.

Another element, however, is that the state only has the prerogative to make this determination if it already enjoys legitimacy. The fixing of the boundary between state and church, between religion and non-religion, is only normatively justified if the state is legitimate in the first place. Acts of meta-jurisdictional boundary drawing only have normative (as opposed to practical legal) authority if the state lives up to whatever conditions there are for legitimacy. Assessments of meta-jurisdictional authority require assessments of legitimacy. We therefore need a full theory of liberal legitimacy in order to be able to determine whether a state in fact has the authority to decide any given boundary question.

Laborde cannot be expected to provide a detailed theory of state legitimacy – her book already covers an extensive topic with several big sub-debates. The general formulation of meta-jurisdictional authority as a function of state legitimacy nevertheless raises one question, which falls squarely within the issue of liberalism and religion. It seems to assume that legitimacy can be ascertained *before* and *independently of* how the state draws the boundaries between religion and non-religion. The state's authority to make the latter kind of decisions depends on its legitimacy, which depends on other qualities (whether it pursues a recognisably liberal conception of justice and does so democratically, cf. p. 162).

But could it not be the case that *whether* the state has liberal legitimacy itself, at least partly, depends on *how* it settles the boundary question? If this is the case, then meta-jurisdictional authority is not a simple function of legitimacy, because there would be a feedback loop from how the state actually decides jurisdictional boundary questions to whether it is in fact legitimate. If so, it would not be possible – contrary to what the quote above might suggest – to determine whether a state is legitimate and therefore has meta-jurisdictional authority *before* and *independently of* how the state draws the boundaries between religion and non-religion.

One might present this possibility as a substantive criticism of Laborde's view: that the relation between legitimacy and boundary drawing is the *reverse* of what she suggests. Libertarians might think that state legitimacy is purely a matter of whether the state respects pre-existing rights and that some of these rights are about non-interference in religion. This would then support church autonomy and the 'New Religious Institutionalism' rather than provide an argument against it.

Chapter 5 of Laborde's book opposes exactly this kind of view. But even if one agrees that libertarianism in general and church autonomy in particular are implausible views, and that liberally legitimate states have meta-jurisdictional sovereignty, *how* the state settles boundary questions still seems relevant to *whether* the state is liberally legitimate. Laborde provides her answer to this question by way of her substantive theory of the justice of exemptions from general laws based on what she calls coherence and competence associational interests.

While I agree with her response to proponents of church autonomy in the first section of Chapter 5 and find her substantive view of freedom of association in the second section plausible, I will end by noting a possible worry about the general *form* of her view. If meta-jurisdictional authority is a function of state legitimacy but state legitimacy in turn partly depends on how the state decides boundary questions, this might lead to a kind of general *regress problem* akin to the democratic boundary problem, that is, that legitimacy depends on boundary-setting, which in turn depends on legitimacy.

The problem arises if there can be *reasonable* disagreement about both a) whether a state is liberally *legitimate* and b) how the *boundary* problem should be settled. Laborde acknowledges the former (p. 165) as well as the latter (p. 163) to be live issues. In such cases, it seems that we cannot say, as Laborde does, that disagreement about boundary drawing is not about jurisdiction but merely about whether a specific decision is just – because the question about whether the state has the requisite meta-jurisdictional authority itself depends on how it settles the boundary question.

Disclosure statement

No potential conflict of interest was reported by the author.

References

Laborde, C. (2017). *Liberalism's Religion*. Cambridge, Mass.: Harvard University Press.
Vallier, K., & D'Agostino, F. (2014). Public justification. E. N.Zalta (ed.), *The stanford encyclopedia of philosophy*. Spring 2014 Edition. Stanford: Metaphysics Research Lab, Stanford University. http://plato.stanford.edu/archives/spr2014/entries/justification-public/

Is epistemic accessibility enough? Same-sex marriage, tradition, and the Bible

Aurélia Bardon

ABSTRACT
In *Liberalism's Religion*, Cécile Laborde argues that a liberal state has to be a justifiable state: state action can only be legitimate if it is publicly justified, that is, if it is based on accessible reasons. These accessible reasons, she argues, are reasons that can be understood by all citizens. She defends a purely epistemic conception of accessibility. On Laborde's account, accessible reasons are identified by particular epistemic features, and not by their substantive content. In this paper, I argue that Laborde's account of epistemic accessibility cannot deliver on its promise of public justification. To illustrate this argument, I examine the case of the prohibition of same-sex marriage and look at two potential reasons that could be used to justify this prohibition: the non-accessible reference to the Bible and the accessible appeal to the value of tradition.

Introduction

Should liberal states be secular? If secularism means the separation of church and state, then not all contemporary liberal states are secular – and, liberal political philosophers have argued, not all liberal states need to be secular in this sense (Ahdar & Leigh, 2004; Brudney, 2005; Laborde, 2013; May, 2012; Modood, 2007). Yet, it does not follow that liberalism is compatible with just any kind of religious establishment or with religiously inspired laws. What is it, then, that states have to do with religion in order to qualify as liberal states?

In Chapter 4 of *Liberalism's Religion*, Cécile Laborde argues that there is some minimal requirement of secularism that is necessary for the liberal understanding of political legitimacy. This minimal secularism has three components: the justifiable state, the inclusive state and the limited state. In this paper, I focus on the first of these three components, the justifiable state. In a justifiable state, state action is only legitimate if it is publicly justified. In order for state action to be publicly justified, Laborde claims that it has to be based on accessible reasons. To the extent that some religious reasons are non-accessible, for instance in the case of direct appeals to God's authority, they are not the kind of reasons that can provide public justification.

In this paper, I argue that Laborde's epistemic account of accessibility (1) cannot deliver on this promise of public justification. To illustrate this argument, I examine the case of the prohibition of same-sex marriage (2) and look at two potential reasons that could be used to justify this prohibition: the non-accessible reference to the Bible and the accessible appeal to the value of tradition. I argue that the epistemic account of accessibility ultimately fails to guarantee public justification: accessible reasons do not necessarily publicly justify decisions in a meaningful way because, based on Laborde's account, reasons violating rules of reasoning can be accessible (3) and because there is no normatively relevant epistemic difference between the premises used in the reference to the Bible and in the appeal to tradition (4).

Laborde's epistemic account of accessibility

Many political philosophers have adopted the principle of public justification as part of the liberal understanding of political legitimacy. In the recent literature, there are, however, important disagreements regarding what this principle entails, and more particularly regarding the definition of the justification requirement: what kind of reasons can be introduced in public debates, and what kind of reasons can provide public justification?

There are three main candidates to define the reasons that should be considered as permissible: shareability, accessibility, and intelligibility.[1] Shareable reasons are those reasons that we can expect all reasonable citizens to endorse; accessible reasons are those reasons that all citizens can assess based on shared evaluative standards; intelligible reasons are those that can be understood in reference to the particular evaluative standards of the person offering the reason. Laborde defends a new interpretation of the accessibility requirement. Her account of the justifiable state has three important features that distinguish it from most other accounts of public justification. These three features express Laborde's ambition to identify an account of public justification that is neither too demanding, nor too permissive, but that still provides a necessary condition for political legitimacy.[2]

First, the duty to provide accessible reasons only applies to state officials and not to ordinary citizens (p. 125).[3] It applies only to them because 'they speak in the name of all' (p. 125). Ordinary citizens, who only speak in their own name, are not under any moral duty to refrain from using non-accessible reasons. This is an important part of Laborde's account of public justification because it provides a way to avoid the powerful objection that requirements of public reason are too demanding, especially for religious citizens. Here, religious citizens do not face any extra burden and 'there is no restriction on views and arguments that ordinary citizens can put forward in public debate' (p. 124). Ordinary citizens, religious or not, can refer to all kinds of reasons, public or non-public, secular or religious.

Second, Laborde's account of the justifiable state starts from actual citizens rather than from idealized citizens. In Rawls's or Quong's accounts, public reason is defined in reference to an idealized conception of citizens, that is, those citizens that can be considered as *reasonable* (Quong, 2011; Rawls, 1993). But the concept of reasonableness is a highly controversial one that is meant to refer to both epistemic rules and ethical content.[4] To avoid such issues, Laborde focuses on actual citizens – or, maybe, on a 'weakly idealized constituency of Members of the Public, such as those formed by minimally rational moral agents' (pp. 277–278, note 16). Contrary to the public reasons of Rawls and Quong, then, Laborde's public reasons, as reasons accessible to actual citizens, or at least to weakly idealized citizens, are not context insensitive and are expected to vary from one place to the other as well as through time. On her account, public reasons are 'the vocabulary, grammar and references of the shared political language of particular societies' (p. 121).

Third, and most importantly, Laborde defends a purely epistemic account of accessibility. Accessible reasons, in this sense, are reasons that share some particular epistemic features. Their substantive content, however, is irrelevant for the question of public justification. Laborde wants to make a very clear distinction between epistemic and substantive wrongs. The state commits an epistemic wrong when 'it does not provide citizens with reasons accessible to them' (p. 119); but the state commits a substantive wrong when it fails to respect all citizens as equal citizens and as self-determining agents (pp. 118–119). For citizens to be respected as self-determining agents, as *democratic reasoners* (p. 118), the state has to present reasons that are accessible to all citizens, that is reasons that all citizens can 'understand and engage with' (p. 119), even when they do not endorse the reason. This is what is required for democratic deliberation to be possible.

What reasons are considered as accessible reasons based on Laborde's definition? Accessible reasons, on her account, are those that can be assessed based on evaluative standards shared by all citizens: not all citizens endorse accessible reasons, but they can all discuss accessible reasons, criticize them, and offer their own accessible counter-reasons. On the other hand, non-accessible reasons are identified as those that 'lack some basic epistemic quality: they are not accessible to common reason' (p. 120). They include notably 'appeals to the authority of a particular God' (p. 118), or to 'personal revelation' (p. 119).

In the justifiable state, the requirement of accessibility is sufficient for public justification. This means that, as long as the reason put forward by the state to support a particular law is accessible, then this law is considered as publicly justified, and it can be concluded that no epistemic wrong has been committed. This, Laborde argues, is only one dimension of political legitimacy: even if accessible reasons are given, it is possible that the state commits a substantive wrong because it violates liberal norms, that is, because it does not meet the requirements of the inclusive state or of the limited state. It meets, however, the requirements of the justifiable state: when the state can present accessible reasons to support its decisions, it provides public justification and guarantees that all citizens are respected as democratic reasoners.

The case of same-sex marriage

Consider a state that does not recognize same-sex marriage but recognizes civil partnerships for same-sex couples, so that same-sex couples get the same legal and fiscal benefits as married couples. The difference, then, is purely symbolic: there is no actual unequal treatment because civil partnership and marriage provide the exact same rights and duties. Is the symbolic difference itself problematic?

On Laborde's account, a liberal state has to be an inclusive state, which means that 'when a social identity is a marker of vulnerability and domination, it should not be symbolically endorsed and promoted by the state' (p. 137). In this case, being married is not a divisive social identity: those who are not married are not considered as second-class citizens. Consequently, the symbolic distinction between marriage and civil partnership does not violate the requirements of the inclusive state.

A liberal state also has to be a limited state, which means that 'when a practice relates to comprehensive ethics, it should not be coercively enforced on individuals' (p. 144). In this case, the law restricting access to marriage to heterosexual couples does not tell people how they should live their life, and so it does not enforce any comprehensive doctrine on them. The individual right to self-determination is not restricted in any way through the symbolic distinction between marriage and civil partnership, and so the requirements of the limited state are also not violated.

In other words, the law itself, that is, the decision to restrict the access to the institution of marriage to heterosexual couples, does not commit any substantive wrong.[5] But has an epistemic wrong been committed? Are the requirements of the justifiable state violated? What kind of reasons can be provided by the state to support this decision?

One obvious example of a non-accessible reason would be the following: *We should not extend the right to marry to same-sex couples because the Bible teaches us that homosexuality is an abomination*. The explicit reference to the Bible as a source of authority is clearly problematic. Whether or not homosexuality is an abomination is a claim that cannot be assessed based on shared evaluative standards. Because of this, it is not part of the language shared by all citizens and it should not be used for public justification. If the only reason provided by state officials to prohibit same-sex marriage is a Biblical statement, then the state is committing an epistemic wrong when it prohibits same-sex marriage. What accessible reasons, then, could there be to prohibit same-sex marriage?

Consider an alternative reason to justify the same decision: *We should not extend the right to marry to same-sex couples, because traditionally, in our society, marriage is defined as the union of a man and a woman.* It is a fact that can be confirmed by empirical evidence, that there is a particular conception of marriage that has been used and legally recognized in Western societies. Is this appeal to the traditional understanding of marriage an accessible reason?

The reason itself is formulated in a generally accessible vocabulary, and it seems that it can be evaluated based on shared standards. But what about the premise, on which the reason is based, that tradition is important, valuable, and that the state should protect it? Is the reference to the value of tradition accessible? Laborde's purely epistemic conception of public justification makes it impossible to consider a reason as non-accessible simply because of the values that it refers to. The idea that tradition is something important does not 'directly appeal to scriptural or theological authority' (p. 123). It is a controversial value – but so are other political values, such as security or welfare, that Laborde counts as public because they can be assessed publicly (p. 122). To exclude appeals to tradition from the set of justificatory reasons, one would have to revise the requirement of accessibility and add a substantive dimension, for instance arguing that tradition is not the *kind of value* that we should appeal to in the public sphere. Laborde, then, either has to accept that an appeal to tradition is an accessible reason that can be used to publicly justify state action or she has to revise the interpretation of the accessibility requirement to add a criterion regarding the substantive content of the reasons and consequently to give up the idea of a purely epistemic conception of public justification.

Laborde explicitly rejects the second option: accessibility remains 'indeterminate about the substantive content and outcome of public reasoning' (p. 121). Substantive considerations, she argues, limit directly the kind of laws that a liberal state can legitimately make (p. 123), but they do not affect the kind of reasons that will be considered as accessible and that can be used for public justification. Consequently, Laborde has to consider appeals to tradition as accessible, and therefore as appropriate for public justification of state action.

This, I believe, is problematic: how would this kind of reason provide any public justification to the decision to prohibit same-sex marriage? In fact, there does not seem to be much difference between the kind of reason that the appeal to tradition is for those who reject the value of tradition and the kind of reason that the reference to the Bible is for those who do not recognize the Bible as a source of moral authority. In both cases, it is clear that the prohibition of same-sex marriage is important for those who believe that the Bible matters for the political decisions that we make, and it is equally clear that the same prohibition is important for those who believe that tradition matters for the political decisions we make. For those who reject both the Bible and tradition as relevant political considerations, both reasons seem to be equally bad.

Admittedly, public justification means that a law has to be supported by public reasons, not that the reasons have to be such that all citizens should endorse them and should agree that the reasons are compelling. There is a crucial distinction between understanding and endorsement of public reasons (pp. 120–122). That those who oppose the prohibition of same-sex marriage believe that the appeal to the Bible or the reference to tradition are *bad* reasons does not suffice to conclude that they are both non-public and that they should not be used in public justification. Laborde argues that the difference between the two reasons remains very important because 'it is one thing to be coerced in the name of reasons one does not understand [...] and quite another to be coerced in the name of reasons that one does not agree with but can engage with' (p. 122). In other words, for those who believe that the prohibition of same-sex marriage is wrong, it is not the same thing to be coerced in the name of the Bible or in the name of tradition. But is it really so? It is far from obvious that there is a significant difference between the two reasons in terms of whether they can provide public justification. In what sense can the reference to tradition, but not the appeal to the Bible, be 'understood and assessed [...] according to common standards' (p. 120)? What kind of shared evaluative standards are available in the first case that would not be equally available in the second?

To see which evaluative standards can be used to assess the reference to the Bible and the appeal to tradition, let us first reconstruct the two reasons. The premises for the tradition-based reason are the following:

P1 – Traditionally, marriage is the union of a man and a woman.
P2 – The state should protect our traditions.
C – The state should not extend to same-sex couples the right to marry.
The premises for the Bible-based reason are the following:
P1 – The Bible tells us that homosexuality is an abomination (Leviticus 18:22).
P2 – The Bible is a reliable source to know what is right and what is wrong.
P3 – The state should prohibit, or at least discourage, wrongful practices.
C – The state should not extend to same-sex couples the right to marry.

What evaluative standards can be used to assess these two reasons, and why could the former but not for the latter be assessed based on shared standards?

Laborde does not provide much information regarding what counts as an evaluative standard, and regarding how to distinguish shared and non-shared standards. Standards of evaluation are the criteria that we use whenever we make a judgment: different standards are at work to decide what is true or false, right or wrong, painful or agreeable, beautiful or ugly, and so on. To assess reasons, two kinds of standards are relevant: epistemic rules of reasoning (3) and other considerations such as moral or metaphysical commitments (4).

Evaluation based on rules of reasoning

It is safe to say that Laborde's shared evaluative standards include at least what Rawls has called the 'forms of reasoning found in common sense, and the methods and conclusions of science when these are not controversial' (Rawls, 1993, p. 224). Logic and science, then, can safely be considered as evaluative standards shared by all citizens. Rules of logic, on the one hand, are used to assess whether the conclusion follows from the premises, or whether it results from a logical fallacy: is there a reasoning error between the premises and the conclusion? Rules of science, on the other hand, apply to factual, empirical statements and can be used to evaluate the validity of premises that are based on such statements: are they, for instance, falsifiable, verifiable, observable, or replicable? Is there a general consensus within the scientific community regarding a particular factual statement?

The critical difference between Rawls and Laborde is the role played by these rules of reasoning in their conceptions of public justification. For Rawls, abiding by these rules of reasoning is a condition of publicity: a reason that would contradict the non-controversial conclusions of science would be considered as non-public and would therefore be excluded from the set of justificatory reasons that can be used to support state action. For Laborde, it seems to be sufficient that a reason *can be assessed* based on shared evaluative standards to be considered as accessible. There is, however, no explicit requirement to actually pass some kind of epistemic test based on such public assessment. The fact that a public assessment is sufficient to conclude that it is a bad reason is irrelevant in Laborde's account of public justification: bad accessible reasons are accessible reasons nonetheless, and therefore, they are a legitimate basis for state action. It then follows that reasons that violate rules of logic or of science can be accessible in Laborde's account of public justification.

Consider the following reasons to support the prohibition of same-sex marriage:

P1 – It is in the best interests of children to be raised by their biological mother and father.

P2 – Children raised by same-sex parents are not raised by their biological mother and father.

P3 – The state should protect the interests of children.

C – The state should not extend to same-sex couples the right to marry.

Let us assume, for the sake of the argument, that the premises are correct. The conclusion, regarding the right to marry, does not follow from the premises that are only concerned with the wellbeing of children: prohibiting same-sex marriage simply has nothing to do with protecting the interests of children. If the premises are correct, then the conclusion should be that same-sex couples should not be allowed to be parents, not that they should not be allowed to get married. Shared rules of reasoning are sufficient, in this case, to conclude that this is a *bad* reason, because it clearly violates rules of logic. Laborde's accessibility requirement is however insufficient to exclude it from the pool of justificatory reasons. In the above example, it is obviously the case that the reason can be assessed in such a way. But are citizens really respected as 'democratic reasoners' (p. 118) when the state uses children's wellbeing as a justification for not recognizing same-sex marriage?

The problem is similar in the case of incorrect factual premises. The first premise in the above example is in fact extremely controversial, and it is contested by most of the available scientific evidence regarding the wellbeing of children raised by same-sex parents. Following Laborde's accessibility requirement, however, this does not make the reason non-accessible. Or consider this even more obvious case: *all environmental policy should be abandoned because climate change is a hoax*. This reason does not violate the rules of logic in the sense that, *if* climate change is not real, then it absolutely makes sense to stop any kind of policy that aims at stopping it. But the premise rejects the non-controversial scientific conclusion that there is a significant, global, and human-induced climate change. In what sense is the state *not* committing an epistemic wrong when it uses such obviously logic-violating or facts-denying reasons? In what sense are such reasons providing meaningful public justification? And why would such a masquerade of public reasoning be relevant in any way for political legitimacy? Because Laborde's account of public justification only requires that reasons are accessible based on shared evaluative standards, but does not impose any minimal threshold of epistemic validity to qualify as a public reason, it cannot provide a distinction between such obviously terrible public reasons and the kinds of reasons that we think states should appeal to when justifying political decisions.

Is there a way for Laborde to avoid this problem and exclude reasons that violate shared rules of logic and of science from the set of justificatory reasons? There is – but she would have to revise her account of epistemic accessibility to make it more demanding than it currently is, to require not only that reasons can be assessed based on shared epistemic rules but that they actually do not violate rules of logic and of science. The relevant and distinctive feature of justificatory reasons, then, would be that they pass a test of minimal epistemic validity.[6]

However, even if such a test of minimal epistemic validity were to be added to Laborde's requirement of accessibility, it would not be sufficient to conclude that the appeal to the Bible is non-accessible whereas the reference to tradition is accessible: it is factually correct that, traditionally, in Western societies, marriage is the union of a man and a woman; but it is also factually correct that the Bible condemns homosexuality. In both cases, the conclusions are logically derived from the sets of premises. Both reasons can be assessed based on shared rules of reasoning in exactly the same way. What distinguishes the reference to the Bible from the appeal to tradition, then, cannot be about rules of reasoning. It has to be about the evaluation of the premises of the reasons.

Moral and metaphysical premises

In most cases, the evaluative standards used to assess and discuss a reason are not limited to rules of logic and science. Shared rules of reasoning play a role in the assessment of all reasons, but ultimate judgments regarding the quality or the force of a reason always depend on many other standards. Rules of logic and science are in particular absolutely pointless to evaluate the moral or metaphysical premises of a reason.

In the case of our two reasons against same-sex marriage, there are no factual mistakes or logical fallacies. The core of the disagreement lies in the premises of the reasons. More particularly, in each case, it is the second premise that is seriously contested:
P2 (*tradition*) – The state should protect our traditions.
P2 (*Bible*) – The Bible is a reliable source to know what is right and what is wrong.

Let us assume that the other premises are generally shared by all citizens and that all citizens can understand that none of the reasons violates the rules of logic and of science. If there is a relevant difference between the two reasons, a distinction that justifies that the reference to tradition is considered as accessible whereas the appeal to the Bible is not, then it has to be somewhere in these two premises. What does it mean to say that (*tradition*) is accessible, but (*Bible*) is not?

There are three different ways mentioned by Laborde to distinguish accessible premises from non-accessible ones: the distinction can be based on (i) the evaluation of the premise, (ii) the shareability of the premise, or on (iii) the source of the premise. All three, I argue, fail to identify a purely epistemic distinction between (*tradition*) and (*Bible*) that would be normatively relevant for the question of public justification.

(i) The evaluation of the premise

The first justification for the distinction is that only (*tradition*) can be subjected to common standards of evaluation. But although factual premises can be subjected to shared standards, it is not clear what this would mean for moral or metaphysical premises. Which standards can we refer to in order to evaluate the claim that the state should protect our traditions, or the claim that the Bible is a reliable source of moral knowledge?

That (*Bible*) cannot be evaluated based on shared standards, i.e. shared standards of evaluation cannot be used to decide if (*Bible*) is something that one should accept as a premise, is pretty straightforward. It is, however, not clear why it would be any different for (*tradition*). To assess the validity of (*tradition*), one needs to refer to a particular conception and evaluation of tradition: why is tradition valuable? To what extent is it morally desirable to guarantee the survival of tradition? When do other values, such as individual liberty, take precedence over the value of tradition? All these questions are the object of deep and reasonable disagreements among citizens: there is no consensual conception of tradition based on which the premise (*tradition*) can be assessed.

Laborde could respond that all citizens share some basic understanding of what tradition is, and that this is enough to conclude that the premise can be assessed based on the shared standard of the concept of tradition itself: (*tradition*) is 'articulated in a language that members of the public can understand and engage with' (p. 119). That might be true – but don't all citizens also share a basic understanding of what morality is, and of what it would mean for the Bible to be the source of it?

More generally, the identification of shared evaluative standards besides rules of reasoning is problematic. Values of equality or fairness, for instance, are very frequently used as standards to assess political reasons. But when should we consider that these are shared and can be appropriately understood as shared evaluative standards? Should it be when all citizens can be expected to *understand* what these values mean, when they all *accept* these values, or when they all *share* a particular conception of these values? Whatever criterion is used, it fails to explain why (*Bible*) makes the reason non-accessible, but (*tradition*) does not. The first option of mere understanding is too weak to justify a distinction because all citizens understand what tradition or morality mean; the two other options of acceptability and shareability are too strong because not all citizens agree that tradition or morality are *good* values, and because they will have many different conceptions of both tradition and morality.

(ii) The shareability of the premise

The second justification for the distinction is that only (*tradition*) is a shared premise. Here, a premise is considered as shared whenever members of the public agree that it is a correct premise, that is, when they endorse the content of the premise. If non-shared premises make the reasons based on them non-accessible, then it follows that accessible reasons are those that are based exclusively on shared premises.

This would successfully explain why (*Bible*) makes the whole reason non-accessible because (*Bible*) is clearly not shared: not all citizens agree that the Bible is a reliable source of moral knowledge. I believe that this is the most plausible way to justify that certain premises make reasons non-accessible. It seems, at times, to fit with how Laborde defines accessibility: 'accessibility articulates what citizens need to share, in particular societies, in order for public deliberation to be possible at all' (p. 121). But requiring the shareability of premises as a condition for the accessibility of reasons is problematic for Laborde because it clashes with two key features of her epistemic account of accessibility.

First, it means that the accessibility of reasons ultimately depends on the substantive content of the reason, and not simply on its epistemic credentials. Shared premises are not distinguished from other premises because of 'some basic epistemic quality' (p. 120). They are simply those that should be, or simply happen to be, at a particular time and for a particular society, the object of a broad consensus: they are not simply understood by all but actually endorsed by all. A reason, consequently, could be accessible if it is based on the premise 'we should treat all as free and equal' but not if it is based on the premise 'we should treat embryos as free and equal'. There is no epistemic difference between the two; the only difference is that the former is shared, whereas the latter is not. Looking into the substantive content of the reason, and more specifically into the content of the premises on which the reason is based, is therefore necessary to know if the reason can be accessible or not. This, however, is incompatible with Laborde's attempt to defend a purely epistemic account of accessibility, 'remaining indeterminate about the substantive content and outcome of public reasoning' (p. 121).

Second, requiring the shareability of premises as a condition for the accessibility of reasons means that the conception of citizens has to be much more idealized than Laborde's 'weakly idealized constituency' (pp. 277–278, note 16). This conception would necessarily include substantive commitments, such that only those who accept certain values (e.g. liberty and equality), and therefore who would accept certain premises (e.g. 'We should treat all as free and equal'), can be considered as reasonable citizens. It is not enough to be a 'minimally rational' moral agent (pp. 277–278, note 16); one also has to share some substantive commitments in the form of certain normative premises.

Finally, it should be noted that requiring shared premises would significantly restrict the set of justificatory reasons: it would rule out the appeal to the Bible as non-accessible, but it would equally rule out the reference to tradition because not all (idealized) citizens would accept the premise (*tradition*).[7]

(iii) The source of the premise

The third justification for the distinction is that only (*tradition*) respects the principle of epistemic abstinence, that is, of 'restraint about questions of deeper foundation and authority' (p. 122). Laborde claims that what her account of accessibility excludes are reasons based on some authority that is not accepted by all citizens. This is, presumably, what explains that when a reason is based on the premise of divine revelation, it is non-accessible. Consequently, reasons can only be accessible if they are based on premises that are not derived from non-shared sources.

Grounding a reason on controversial sources of moral authority is, admittedly, problematic. But the issue with this third justification is that it implies that simply remaining silent regarding the source of the premise would suffice to make the premise, and therefore the reason itself, accessible. If one wants to legitimately use moral or religious beliefs to support any kind of political decision, then one only has to omit to mention the foundation for these beliefs. It is, however, difficult to see why this would guarantee the accessibility of reasons and why this would provide public justification in any meaningful sense.

The problem appears quite clearly in Laborde's example of two statements: 'God wishes us to treat all as free and equal' and 'we should treat all as free and equal' (p. 122). The two statements have identical substantive contents, but whereas the first one provides a particular (and non-accessible) foundation to justify the content, the second does not and simply avoids any mention of a deeper foundation. Laborde concludes that the first statement is 'not accessible in public reason' (p. 122), whereas the second one is, precisely because it applies 'restraint about questions of deeper foundation and authority' (p. 122). The distinction between the content and the source of the reason is crucial to this argument, and this distinction explains why reasons that are derived from religious doctrines can be accessible reasons: reasons can be accessible even when the source of the reason is non-accessible, if the content of the reason is 'detachable' (p. 126) and can be assessed independently of the non-accessible doctrine that it originates from.

There is, however, something deeply troubling about this. First, there is actually an important difference between the two statements mentioned by Laborde: the first statement provides a *reason*, but the second one does not. In both cases, we are told that all people should be treated as free and equal. What if anyone were to ask why we should treat all people as free and equal? The first statement explains that this is what God wants and expects from us; the second does not say anything about why this should be the case. In other words, the first statement is a reason, but not an accessible one; the second statement is accessible, but it is not a reason. If all references to the source and foundation of premises are removed, what kind of *reasons* are we left with?

Second, the restraint about questions of foundation is a very low threshold for accessibility. It does not actually rule out any particular reason but only requires to superficially change the way a reason is presented: simply saying 'we should' instead of 'God wants us to', or referring to natural law rather than to divine law, would be enough to pass the test of accessibility. It suffices to reframe non-accessible reasons, without changing their content at all, to make them accessible. Statements such as 'we should treat embryos as moral persons', 'we should recognize different gender roles', or 'we should protect our religious identity' would be considered as accessible because they do not say anything about deeper foundation. They are not epistemically different from the statement 'we should treat all as free and equal'. One can only distinguish between 'we should treat embryos as moral persons' and 'we should treat all as free and equal' based on a thick substantive account of public justification, not with a thin epistemic one.

The restraint about questions of foundation makes public argumentation impossible: there is no counter-argument for 'we should treat embryos as moral persons' if one cannot go into questions of foundation. One simply accepts the premise or one rejects it. It cannot guarantee public justification: what difference in terms of justification does it make if the reason provided by the state for the prohibition of same-sex marriage is 'because this is how we have always done things around here', 'because this is the right thing to do', or 'because God told me so'? The argument that only reasons that make no reference to any deep foundation could be accessible does successfully explain why *(tradition)* is accessible whereas *(Bible)* is not. But it fails to explain why the appeal to tradition actually provides a meaningful, public justification for the prohibition of same-sex marriage, to those who believe that this decision and the premise *(tradition)* on which it is based are both wrong. In other words, it is hard to see why they should feel more respected as democratic reasoners with a reason based on *(tradition)* than with a reason based on *(Bible)*, although they reject both premises equally. Or, to use a different example, it is hard to see why there is public justification for the prohibition of abortion if the reason provided by the state is that we should respect embryos as moral persons, but not if the reason provided by the state is that, according to a religious text, embryos should be respected as moral persons. It seems highly controversial to argue that such a distinction could be relevant in any way for political legitimacy.

Conclusion

In this paper, I have argued that Laborde's epistemic account of accessibility ultimately fails to provide public justification. The examination of two potential reasons for the prohibition of same-sex marriage shows that such a purely epistemic account is insufficient: whatever distinction it provides between accessible and non-accessible reasons is irrelevant for the question of public justification. The epistemic account is insufficient because it does not require that accessible reasons pass a test of minimal epistemic validity in reference to rules of reasoning and because it does not take substantive considerations into account to distinguish between accessible and non-accessible premises. This might suffice to identify statements formulated in a generally accessible vocabulary, but it does not suffice to identify public reasons that actually have some justificatory bite for all citizens, including for those who reject both the reason and the decision that it supports.

Notes

1. For a discussion of these three requirements, see Vallier (2014).
2. On Laborde's account, public justification is not the only condition for political legitimacy.
3. Unless otherwise indicated, page references are to Laborde (2017).
4. On the issues raised by the concept of reasonableness in political liberalism, see notably Wenar (1995), Moore (1996), and Estlund (1998).
5. There is no substantive wrong because of the assumption that equal rights are guaranteed. However, if homosexuality was criminalized or if same-sex couples could not benefit from the same rights as other couples, then the state would clearly commit a substantive wrong.
6. It should be noted that it is possible to interpret Laborde's accessibility as requiring such a test of minimal epistemic validity already. Laborde's conception of accessibility is based on Vallier's definition: 'A's reason R_A is accessible for members of the public if and only if members of the public regard R_A as epistemically justified for A according to common evaluative standards' (Vallier, 2014, p. 108). If so, then reasons violating shared rules of logic and of science would not be actually justified according to these same standards, and consequently such reasons should be considered as non-accessible. But Laborde never explicitly acknowledges that the accessibility requirement restricts the set of justificatory reasons in such a way, and she does not discuss directly the question of empirically or scientifically false claims. There is, therefore, some ambiguity around it.
7. It might be argued that what is required is not that all citizens accept the premise 'The state should protect our traditions', but that all citizens accept only that tradition has *some* value. I am not sure whether reasonable citizens would actually all accept that tradition has some value. Nevertheless, the idea that tradition is a shared value in that sense seems less controversial than the idea that the Bible (or religion) is a shared value, and so it might successfully distinguish between (*tradition*) and (*Bible*). That being said, this is an interpretation of the shareability of the premise that is anyway not available to Laborde for the same reasons that the more demanding interpretation of the shareability of the premise is not available: it would not be a purely epistemic account of accessibility, and it would require a more demanding conception of idealized citizens.

Disclosure statement

No potential conflict of interest was reported by the author.

References

Ahdar, R., & Leigh, I. (2004). Is establishment consistent with religious freedom. *McGill Law Journal, 49*, 635–681.
Brudney, D. (2005). On noncoercive establishment. *Political Theory, 33*(6), 812–839.
Estlund, D. (1998). The insularity of the reasonable: Why political liberalism must admit the truth. *Ethics, 108*(2), 252–275.
Laborde, C. (2013). Political liberalism and religion: On separation and establishment. *Journal of Political Philosophy, 21*(1), 67–86.
Laborde, C. (2017). *Liberalism's Religion*. Cambridge, MA: Harvard University Press.
May, S. C. (2012). Democratic legitimacy, legal expressivism, and religious establishment. *Critical Review of International Social and Political Philosophy, 15*(2), 219–238.
Modood, T. (2007). *Multiculturalism: A Civic Idea*. Cambridge: Polity.
Moore, M. (1996). On reasonableness. *Journal of Applied Philosophy, 13*(2), 167–178.
Quong, J. (2011). *Liberalism without perfection*. Oxford: Oxford University Press.
Rawls, J. (1993). *Political liberalism*. New York, NY: Columbia University Press.
Vallier, K. (2014). *Liberal politics and public faith: Beyond separation*. New York, NY: Routledge.
Wenar, L. (1995). Political liberalism: An internal critique. *Ethics, 106*(1), 32–62.

Defending broad neutrality

Jeffrey W. Howard

> **ABSTRACT**
> This paper interrogates Cécile Laborde's account of the proper role of religion in the liberal state. It begins by examining Laborde's claims that prevailing liberals are not committed to *broad* neutrality about the good, but rather only *restricted* neutrality about the good—and that they are right to do so. It argues against Laborde on both exegetical and substantive grounds. It then turns to Laborde's minimalist conception of secularism, according to which the state must be *justifiable, inclusive,* and *limited,* and it argues that it is not sufficiently demanding. Finally, it argues that the classical liberal presumption of skepticism toward religious establishment is warranted.

Introduction

Cécile Laborde's powerful new work, *Liberalism's Religion*, challenges liberal political philosophers to rethink our complacent assumptions about the restricted place of religion in a just society. *Pace* prevailing wisdom, Laborde contends that the familiar hostility of liberal egalitarians to religion in politics—and to religious establishment in particular—is misplaced. That hostility, she argues, is fueled by a seemingly attractive but pernicious myth at the very heart of liberal political philosophy: namely, that the state ought to be neutral toward all questions of value that lie beyond political justice. In Chapter 3 of the book, she exposes the myth for what it is, showing that some of the most important liberal egalitarians are not, in fact, committed to this thesis. In Chapter 4, she traces the implications of that finding for the role of religion in public affairs, contending that the state must be neutral only toward particular features of religion, rather than religion *in toto*. In so doing, she furnishes a novel conception of what secularism is and what it minimally requires—one compatible with certain forms of religious establishment.

Here my aim is to cast doubt on these particular claims. I begin by examining Laborde's discussion in Chapter 3, raising concerns about the distinction between broad and restricted neutrality as it arises in her discussions of Ronald Dworkin and Jonathan Quong, and suggesting that we should be more sympathetic to broad neutrality than Laborde argues. I then turn to Chapter 4, arguing that Laborde's minimalist conception of secularism—according to which the state must be *justifiable, inclusive,* and *limited* —is not sufficiently demanding. My criticism focuses on Laborde's interpretation of what justifiability requires, contending that the idea of *accessibility*, which is central to her view, has almost no normative significance. I will also reject Laborde's contention that a state with religious establishment could nevertheless qualify as *inclusive*; in so doing, I defend the classical liberal skepticism toward religious establishment. Ultimately I will suggest that while Laborde is right that certain states with established religions may be legitimate, this is not because the justice of religious establishment is a matter of reasonable disagreement; it is not. Rather, it is simply because religious establishment often only qualifies as a *mild* injustice, and thus does not invalidate the government's right to rule.

Rethinking restricted vs. broad neutrality
Political liberalism and reasonable disagreement

A defining feature of liberalism as a political philosophy is its refusal to take a stand on a variety of contested questions—about the meaning of the universe, about the proper purposes of human life, about the existence of God. The government, liberals hold, should be *neutral* about such vexed matters. So goes the familiar slogan. But what, exactly, is the defining feature of these matters that makes them inappropriate subjects of the state's consideration? In virtue of *what* is it objectionable for the state to take a stand on them, or justify its laws on their basis?

In Chapter 3 of *Liberalism's Religion*, Laborde demonstrates that once we press prevailing liberal egalitarian theories on this question, it becomes clear that the aspiration of 'state neutrality' toward comprehensive conceptions of value is far more restricted than commonly recognized. The strategy of this chapter involves examining three views within liberal political theory: one by Ronald Dworkin; a second by Christopher Eisgruber and Lawrence Sager; and a third, Rawlsian view, defended by Jonathan Quong. Through a close analysis of their writings, she explores how what may seem like a commitment to a capacious understanding of neutrality only amounts to a far more restricted understanding.

Because Laborde builds her own approach in Chapter 4 out of elements of these three views, it is crucial to examine whether these views are, in fact, committed to restricted neutrality rather than broad neutrality. And of course, even if she is right that they are so committed, it remains a further question whether such a commitment is plausible. I want to raise doubts about both issues. First, I'll concentrate on the exegetical issue, before turning to the substantive question. For the sake of space, I'll focus specifically on Laborde's discussion of political liberalism, and especially her claim that political liberalism (as defended by Jonathan Quong) is only committed to restricted neutrality.

Laborde's claim is that Quong's theory 'does not successfully rule out moderate perfectionism' (p. 99)—a serious charge indeed, given that his book is entitled *Liberalism Without Perfection*. In the chapter of Quong's book on which Laborde focuses the puzzle with which Quong is wrestling is this: if reasonable disagreement about the good life means that we should exclude considerations of the good from public justification, why doesn't reasonable disagreement about justice mean that we should exclude considerations of justice from public justification? Quong's answer invokes a distinction between *justificatory* disagreements—in which we are reasonably disagreeing about the implications of a common ideal, such as liberal justice—from *foundational* disagreements—in which we lack a common basis for justifying our positions (Quong, 2010, p. 193).

On the basis of this distinction, Laborde interprets Quong to be committed to the following claim: 'The salient feature of ideals about the good is...that they are (epistemically) non-shareable' (p. 97). Laborde's central insight is that this is not necessarily the case; it appears that there are some ideals of the good that *are* shareable and indeed shared. Thus if we are to preserve the idea that claims about the good life should be excluded from public justification, the distinction between justificatory and foundational disagreement cannot account for this.[1]

Laborde is right that the distinction between justificatory and foundational disagreement cannot itself account for the broad neutrality of Quong's political liberalism. But this would be a decisive objection to Quong's theory only if its anti-perfectionism depended on this distinction alone. But it manifestly doesn't.[2] Quong's primary reason for rejecting perfectionism is *not* the epistemic claim that ideals of the good are not amenable to agreement. Rather, it is the *normative* claim that imposing ideals of the good through law is incompatible with respect for citizens as free and equal. Specifically, it is incompatible with respect for citizens' *second moral power*, 'the capacity to form, revise, and rationally pursue their own conception of the good' (Quong, 2010, p. 101). Perfectionist policies are wrongful because they fail to respect persons' prerogative to pursue their own good in their own way. Specifically, Quong argues that perfectionist policies are wrong because they are *paternalistic*: they hinge on 'a negative judgement about the ability of others to run their own lives' (2012, p. 74). This argument simply does not presuppose the previous epistemic argument, even if it is consistent with it.[3]

Quong has a further reason for rejecting perfectionism, even of a moderate variety. *Such legislation is wholly unrelated to the moral aims that justify the state's authority in the first place.* On Quong's view, the justification of state authority is the natural duty of justice, and the state secures its legitimacy from the way in which it enables citizens to satisfy the duties of justice they owe to others (2012, pp. 126ff). An authority so conceived simply lacks the prerogative to make and enforce laws that help people live better lives.

Quong could, of course, help himself to an alternative theory of state authority that is, in principle, amenable to the idea that a central purpose of government is to help people lead good lives.[4] But that theory would be precisely the perfectionist, service conception of authority defended by Joseph Raz—precisely the view that Quong's book aims to defeat. So the only way for Quong to accept that the state has the right to enforce moderate perfectionist policies is to alter his fundamental theory of state authority. And if he were to do that, he would cease, following Raz, to be even a defender of *restricted* neutrality; he'd have to give up on neutrality altogether. That is the logical implication of Laborde's criticism of Quong. Because it is an implausible implication, it raises the question of whether we can interpret Quong in a better way—one that enables him to resist the specter of perfectionism. I have argued that we can.

Thus even if citizens broadly agree about a common justificatory framework about the good—even if they discover that they share a common ethical commitment about what a good life involves—this alone does not make it justifiable to impose it through law.[5] The point of state power is not to improve citizens' conformity with their own good. It is to enable them to discharge their natural duties of justice.

In sum, while Laborde is right that the distinction between justificatory and foundational disagreement has limited significance, it does not therefore follow that political liberals must accept moderate perfectionism. Indeed, I believe this shows that political liberals would do well to ground their antiperfectionism in the ideals of freedom and equality, and of respect for the two moral powers, rather than in the nature of different kinds of disagreement. Quong needlessly invites Laborde's attack by emphasizing the latter.[6]

Personal ethics and impersonal value

Suppose, however, that Laborde is right: prevailing versions of liberal-egalitarianism, when scrutinized, only require moderate perfectionism. Still, it is worth inquiring what should follow from that conclusion. Even if Laborde is right as a matter of exegesis, it remains a further question whether moderate perfectionism is plausible. So consider another thinker that Laborde examines: Ronald Dworkin. As Laborde shows, Dworkin believes that the state should be neutral toward competing conceptions of *personal ethics*: 'convictions about the importance of human life or of achievement in human life' (2018, p. 71). Convictions about 'impersonal value'—about the intrinsic value of forests, or artwork, or knowledge itself—are perfectly acceptable bases for state action. The claim that Dworkin is committed to restricted, rather than broad neutrality, rests precisely upon this distinction.

Is this actually a plausible distinction? Let us grant that Laborde succeeds in making the exegetical point that this was, in fact, Dworkin's distinction (pp. 76–77). But given that Laborde embraces it for the purposes of her definition of a *limited state* in Chapter 4, it is not enough that this be the exegetically accurate interpretation of Dworkin. The distinction needs to survive scrutiny. I doubt that it does. Consider the idea that the state should fund opera. Why should it fund opera? One possibility is to appeal straightforwardly to the principle that *opera is intrinsically valuable* (say, in virtue of the way in which it powerfully harnesses music to explore important questions in the human experience). But a second possibility is to appeal to the principle that *one ought to appreciate opera because it is intrinsically valuable*. The first is a statement of impersonal, intrinsic value; the second is a statement of what people ought to do in order to live the kind of life that responds to intrinsic value in the world. Are these statements really so different? Note that the second statement does not reduce opera to something an agent should do to increase her own utility. It is a statement about how a proper human life, one responsive to the value in the world, should be lived. Indeed, *most* conceptions of the good have this feature; most are accounts of what has value in the world and how we ought to respond to that value.

Is Laborde actually convinced that there is a crucial difference between these two principles? I cannot see what the crucial difference is; the second seems plainly entailed by the first. If Laborde is prepared to give Dworkin's distinction between 'ethical convictions that are central to personality, like convictions about abortion, and other convictions, that...are not' (2004, p. 358) the pivotal role that she does toward the end of Chapter 4, we need a more robust defense of it than Dworkin provides.

Rethinking religious establishment

Laborde believes that moderate perfectionism is acceptable at the bar of liberal justice. Because she believes that, she believes that some forms of religious establishment are acceptable. I now want to argue that even if we grant that moderate perfectionism can be acceptable (setting aside my skepticism so far), we should retain the conventional liberal hostility toward religion in public life—specifically, hostility toward the use of exclusively religious arguments[7] in public justification, and toward religious establishment.

In Chapter 4, Laborde advances the argument that 'when religious ideas and practices do not meet the features that make state establishment impermissible, then the state may endorse and affirm them' (p. 115). Religious ideas and practices are inappropriate in public life when they are *inaccessible, divisive,* or *comprehensive.* Conversely, religious ideas and practices can be fully appropriate so long as they do not compromise the state's status as *justifiable, inclusive,* or *limited.* Laborde thus concludes:

> There is more variation in legitimate state-religion relationships than liberal egalitarians have recognized...Symbolic recognition of religion, conservative laws in matters of bio-ethics, religious accommodations from general laws, and religious references in public debate are not incompatible with minimal secularism and liberal legitimacy (pp. 116–117).

This does not, she thinks, mean that the *best* theory of liberal justice will endorse such policies. Her point, instead, is that there can be 'reasonable disagreement' about such matters (p. 153).

I want to criticize this position by scrutinizing the first two components of Laborde's conception of minimal secularism: first, the idea that a secular state must be *justifiable*; and second, the idea that a secular state must be *inclusive*.

The justifiable state

A state, Laborde contends, must be *justifiable* to those it governs. But what does justifiability mean? Laborde's strategy in this chapter is to take the basic impulses of the liberal views surveyed in Chapter 3 to construct her own vision of what liberal justice minimally requires. The idea that a liberal state must be *justifiable* is evidently inspired by Quong's Rawlsian view. But Laborde deviates from this view substantially, and in ways that render her position less plausible than it could be.

Steering a middle course between the requirement that reasons for coercive laws be *intelligible* to all those coerced, and the requirement that reasons for coercive laws be *endorsed* (and thus *shared*) by all those coerced, Laborde defends the proposal that reasons for coercive laws be *accessible* to all those coerced. She argues that *accessible* reasons are reasons that 'can be understood and assessed, but need not be endorsed according to common standards' (p. 120).[8] By making accessibility the defining virtue of public deliberation, Laborde defends what she calls 'a thinly epistemic theory of public reason' (p. 119).

Why is accessibility normatively significant? Laborde argues that the state perpetrates what she describes as an 'epistemic wrong' (p. 118) when it coerces citizens 'in the name of reasons that they do not understand and cannot engage with'. In such cases, 'they are not respected as *democratic reasoners*' (p. 118). But why? Consider two cases. In the first case, a fanatic proposes a law that would execute all members of my ethnic group, on the grounds that she has had a personal revelation from God enjoining her to do so. In the second case, a fanatic proposes the same law me on the grounds that she has a moral duty to protect the political community by eliminating dangerous elements, which she has determined by working through arguments about the demands of her religion's holy book. Let's grant that she wrongs me, all-things-considered, in both cases—something Laborde would obviously accept. Laborde nevertheless seems to think that the first case is worse, since the reasons are not accessible to me; in this case, I cannot understand and assess her reasons for acting. The epistemic inaccessibility, Laborde thinks, *wrongs me* epistemically. Thus while I have a complaint, at least in the second case I can say: 'I'm about to be murdered – but at least I'm being respected as a democratic reasoner!'

This strikes me as unpersuasive. What difference does it really make that the wrongdoer's reasons are accessible? Note that Laborde places no substantive, moral constraints on what counts as accessible; it is a wholly epistemic criterion. Thus reasons derived from New Natural Law are accessible since they are 'based on inferences that require no appeal to special knowledge such as divine revelation' (p. 127). But—to change the example—I cannot see what difference this epistemic fact should make to a gay citizen about to be imprisoned for violating conservative sexual rules. What difference does it make whether the state is imprisoning him because of inaccessible divine revelation, or fully accessible inference on the basis of some manifestly mistaken but nevertheless comprehensible piece of reasoning? It's all injustice to him.

Laborde anticipates this worry by noting that the accessibility condition is simply 'an epistemic constraint on the inputs of public debate'—so while it is necessary, it 'is not a sufficient condition of liberal legitimacy' (p. 129). But what I question is why it should be listed as a separate condition at all. Why does Laborde think it is even *pro tanto* wrong to coerce a person on basis of beliefs that are inaccessible? Laborde notes that the accessibility condition 'identifies what kinds of reasons can enter the "permissibility pool" but does not specify which reasons are conclusive enough to provide a full justification for public policy and law' (p. 130). But why is it permitted in the pool to begin with? The idea seems to be motivated, of course, by the conviction that there is something *additionally* wrong about coercing someone on the basis of reasons (s)he cannot even comprehend. Yet my example cases raise doubts about precisely that point. The arguments in *Mein Kampf* are publicly accessible—they are not based on revelation or testimony. But this fact seems to make no difference at all to whether they ought to be part of the 'permissibility pool.' If the permissibility pool is so broad as to include all this, accessibility is reduced to a trivial precondition (just as 'All reasons must be explicable using human language' would be a trivial precondition). The normative significance of this epistemic condition is thus minimal at best, nonexistent at worst.[9]

Laborde could well reply that it would be a serious cost to her theory to eliminate talk of accessibility. But there is a serious question as to whether she needs it at all. My own suggestion to her is that the justifiability condition of a legitimate state—Laborde's first criterion, which she casts the notion of accessibility to play—is simply a function of her second and third criteria (inclusiveness and liberty). In other words, we want an inclusive state—one that supports the civic equality of citizens—and we want a limited state—one that supports the freedom of citizens—and that insofar as the state accomplishes these goals, it is justifiable to them. This is not to say that we should abandon talk of public justification; it is simply to say that public justification is a matter of attunement with the ideals of inclusiveness and liberty. In Rawlsian terms, a policy or argument is publicly justified just in case it expresses respect for citizens as free and equal—as bearers of the two moral powers, who have a claim to fair terms of social cooperation.[10]

The inclusive state

I now want to examine Laborde's second feature of a secular state. On her view, '[w]hen a social identity is a marker of vulnerability and domination, it should not be symbolically endorsed and promoted by the state' (p. 150). Because religion is not always such a marker, Laborde argues, symbolic recognition of religion cannot be ruled out as incompatible with liberal-egalitarian values. Developing the insights defended by Eisgruber and Sager, Laborde's thesis is that religious establishment is problematic only when it has the effect of disparaging certain groups and undermining civic equality—perpetrating what Nussbaum calls 'expressive subordination' of those who do not share the official religion (2011, p. 135). When it does not do this, however, religious establishment is wholly unproblematic. Laborde thus gives us the example of a hypothetical state—*Divinitia*. In *Divinitia*, the government 'symbolically recognises one religion, but not in a way that infringes on the equal citizenship of non-adherents' p. 151). So, the state does not award special material benefits to the adherents of that religion, it does not prefer them for public offices, and it does not actively educate schoolchildren to regard the official religion as one they should adopt.

I have two objections to this argument. First, even if is true that there are certain countries—for example, Madagascar and Senegal (p. 142)—in which religion is not divisive, this is not sufficient to demonstrate that liberals' *presumptive* skepticism toward religious establishment is unwarranted (as Laborde says it is when criticizing Kymlicka on p. 143). Normative reflection on history gives us excellent reason to be *prima facie* skeptical of even 'merely' symbolic establishment. In the vast preponderance of societies, state recognition of religion is divisive. Insofar as we embrace not simply a *liberal* but also a *republican* approach to our institutional design—ensuring that the institutions we create will be *robust* in their protection of citizens' status as free and equal—we have reasons to worry about the reasons that ordinarily motivate human beings to establish religions.

This objection applies most forcefully to cases in which citizens are offering a *new* proposal to establish a religion. It is extraordinarily difficult to imagine a context in which (a) citizens are so religiously devoted that they insist the state symbolically recognize *their* religion, and yet in which (b) those who are adhered to the religions would be wholly untroubled. Of course, the psychological fact that they are troubled is not sufficient to establish a legitimate complaint. But given the kinds of reasons that have motivated human beings to unite religion and state,[11] there is excellent reason to conclude that religion is presumptively illegitimate as an object of state symbolic endorsement.[12] Even granting, then, that it is not *necessarily* illegitimate, there is a demanding burden of proof required for anyone proposing religious establishment. Religious minorities can be forgiven for worrying whether 'merely symbolic' recognition of a majority religion could slip someday into coercive support for that religion.

My second reason for opposing religious establishment is simple, and recalls the argument made in the previous section about political liberalism and state authority. According to numerous liberals, the fundamental justification of the state's authority—and our obligation to obey it—is the natural duty of justice. The state has authority over us, on this view, because by complying with it, we are better positioned to satisfy the duties of justice we owe to others; we better succeed at treating one another as free and equal moral agents.[13] On a liberal view, the purpose of state authority is to realize just institutions, which secure citizens with their fair share of liberties and opportunities with which they can then pursue their conceptions of a good life. It rightly engages in coercion for this purpose.

Yet the proposal that the state should take sides in questions of religious truth is unconnected to this purpose, and it is extremely difficult to see how it advances it. In other words: how does the state get the authority to take sides on religious questions? It is difficult to see why citizens would grant the state the authority to expend its symbolic and material resources 'taking a stand' on religious matters. Perhaps there are such reasons—for example, by taking a stand on religious questions, then state facilitates religious homogeneity, which in turn stabilizes the regime. This may well be empirically so. But it is difficult to see why citizens who *deny* the official religion ought nevertheless not to be insulted by this—to view it as a case of 'stability for the wrong reasons'. Surely they should. Insofar as religious pluralism is the free outcome of reason under free institutions, it is very difficult to see why citizens, viewing one another as free and equal, would nevertheless authorize the state to champion one religion over others.

This all leads to a crucial final point. Intuitively, I think we all should agree with Laborde that *Divinitia* is, indeed, a legitimate state. But Laborde seems to rely on the popular idea that a state is legitimate if it is regulated by a reasonable conception of justice—a conception within the family of reasonable political conceptions. Laborde's distinctive aim is to show that a reasonable conception of political justice could authorize religious establishment under certain conditions. If the arguments I have advanced are right, I believe we should be genuinely skeptical about that. But I think it's still true that a state like *Divinitia* is legitimate—it retains the right to make and enforce law over its territory—for the simple reason that it is *sufficiently just*. While it contains injustices, they are not egregious injustices, even if they are nevertheless undeniably unjust by any reasonable view. *Divinitia* is, in the terminology of *The Law of Peoples*, a decent society (Rawls, 2001). Internal efforts to overthrow the government, or external efforts at regime change, would be morally impermissible. And that's because religious establishment simply need not be considered as heinously unjust as most liberals tend to suggest. The natural duty of justice would enjoin us to continue to support that state and, of course, work to increase its justice. So while religious establishment is, I have argued, likely beyond the pale of reasonable disagreement, a state with it need not be considered illegitimate.

Notes

1. Quong recognizes the possibility of deep agreement among citizens about the good life (2010, p. 254), but does not think this possibility has the implications Laborde argues it does.
2. See also Quong 2012, p. 56. Laborde appears to recognize this on p. 130, note 44. But this deflates the force of her criticism.
3. As others have argued, one can reject the burdens of judgement with respect to questions of the good life—since one believes one's preferred comprehensive doctrine is obviously correct—and *still* be wholeheartedly committed to the idea that individuals have the moral right to decide their own paths in life for themselves. See, for example, Wenar, 1995, pp. 41–48, and Nussbaum, 2011; p. 20.

4. This is, of course, incompatible with the Dworkinian view that Laborde also endorses—but this just goes to show the difficult .
5. It might be replied that it is justifiable if there is genuine consensus on it. This is unlikely, given the burdens of judgement, but let's suppose it's possible. Even so, there are two Rawlsian replies. First, we must view ourselves as possessing the prerogative to alter our views about the good life. Even if it would be permissible for me to create a mechanism whereby I am threatened with punishment unless I comply with my own preferred conception of the good life—as an act of self-binding—it would be wrong of me to insist that others undertake similar self-binding. A society in which citizens remain free to alter their conception of the good life does not use its criminal law to enforce conformity with a particular conception, even if the conception that is presently popular. Second, and more controversially, the state has a duty to ensure that children are free to select whatever justice-consistent conception of the good they choose when they become adults; a society that has selected its preferred conception of the good and crafted its basic structure along its lines arguably contravenes this duty.
6. His comments on the possibility of a moderate perfectionism, in particular, court this attack (2012, pp. 215ff)—in my view, unnecessarily.
7. By 'exclusively religious arguments,' I mean arguments that do not have a public analogue, as per Rawls's famous proviso in Rawls, 2005, pp. 783–784. By public analogue, I do not simply mean an argument that is 'accessible' in Laborde's highly minimal sense. Following Rawls, an argument is public when it is cast in terms of one of the members of the family of reasonable political conceptions of justice.
8. See further discussion in Vallier and D'Agostino, 2014. Note that Laborde's definition of intelligibility appears weaker than Vallier and D'Agostino's. For them, 'A's reason R_A is accessible to the public if and only if all members of the public regard R_A as justified for A according to common evaluative standards.' I believe my objection would stand even if Laborde employed Vallier and D'Agostino's definition, but it would require some modification.
9. Two reviewers helpfully suggest that these examples concern cases in which the policy in question is obviously wrong. If we consider cases in which the policy is permissible, but the proffered justification is inaccessible, we might think that there is, in fact, a separate, epistemic wrong at work. For example, suppose that a just environmental policy is justified by a speaker on the grounds that his deity (whom I do not recognize) enjoins us to protect the planet. Does the speaker thereby disrespect me? I think the answer is no, but precisely because there is a plausible public justification for the policy in question (see note 7). My point is simply that it is implausible to think that an injustice perpetrated on the basis of inaccessible reasons (in Laborde's minimal sense) is *worse* than an injustice perpetrated on the basis of accessible reasons. The properties that render the policy or conduct wrongful determine the gravity of the wrongness, not the arguments that the wrongdoer utters to rationalize them.
10. One reviewer notes that a policy might be consistent with liberty and inclusivity, yet fail accessibility—for example, a proposal to fund the arts justified on the basis of the argument that doing so glorifies God. My claim is that so long as the policy can be justified on the basis of a commitment to liberty and

inclusivity, the fact that various citizens articulate private comprehensive reasons why they support the policy need not be construed as disrespectful to others, precisely because an argument is available in terms of liberty and inclusivity.
11. All of which have concerned giving members of the preferred religion a symbolic or material advantage—why would they spend so much energy advocating for establishment of their preferred religion if it *didn't* have this effect?.
12. As one reviewer notes, we might think that a state can symbolically establish a religion without sending the message that it is the correct religion. I find this difficult to accept.
13. This duty is discussed in Rawls, 2005, pp. 99–100, 115, 293–301, and 334, as well as in Waldron, 1993; Stilz, 2009. And see Quong, 2010; p. 128.

Acknowledgments

I am grateful to all who participated in our UCL symposium on *Liberalism's Religion*, especially Aurelia Bardon and Cécile Laborde. I am also indebted to the two referees, whose comments improved this paper greatly.

References

Dworkin, R. 2004. "Ronald Dworkin Replies." In J. Burley (Ed.), *Dworkin and his Critics*. Oxford: Blackwell
Laborde, C. (2018). *Liberalism's Religion*. Cambridge, MA: Harvard University Press.
Nussbaum, M. (2011). Political Liberalism and Perfectionist Liberalism. *Philosophy & Public Affairs*, 39, 3–45.
Quong, J. (2010). *Liberalism without Perfection*. New York: Oxford University Press.
Quong, J. (2012). Liberalism Without Perfection: Replies to Gaus, Colburn, Chan, and Bocchiola. *Philosophy and Public Issues*, 2, 51–79.
Rawls, J. (1971/1999). *A Theory of Justice* (revised ed.). Cambridge, MA: Harvard University Press.
Rawls, J. (2005). *Political Liberalism*. New York: Columbia University Press.
Rawls, J. (2001). *The Law of Peoples*. Cambridge, MA: Harvard University Press.
Stilz, A. (2009). *Liberal Loyalty: Freedom, Obligation, and the State*. Princeton: Princeton University Press.
Vallier, K., & D'Agostino, F. (2014). Public Justification. In E. N. Zalta (Ed.), *The Stanford Encyclopedia of Philosophy*. Stanford, CA: The Metaphysics Research Lab, Stanford University. Retrieved from https://plato.stanford.edu/archives/spr2014/entries/justification-public/
Waldron, J. (1993). Special Ties and Natural Duties. *Philosophy & Public Affairs*, 22, 3–30.
Wenar, L. (1995). Political liberalism: an internal critique. *Ethics*, *106*, 32–62. doi:10.1086/293777

On *Liberalism's Religion*

Jean L. Cohen

> **ABSTRACT**
> This chapter addresses two crucial issues raised by Laborde's superb *Liberalism's Religion*. The first pertains to where the liberal democratic modern state draws the line between the self-governing prerogatives of religious nomos communities and their regulation by the civil law; the second pertains to the prerogative of the state to do the relevant line drawing. Theorists concerned with religious freedom focus on the first set of questions under the rubric of 'accommodation.' The issue is unfair discrimination. I focus on Laborde's approach to the second. This is again an important issue due to the recent revival of jurisdictional political pluralism: an approach that challenges the supremacy of the civil law and of the authority of the sovereign state over domestic religious authorities. I suggest more work must be done to parry those challenges.

Introduction

Liberalism's Religion is an important addition to contemporary debates over religion, secularism, liberalism, and the state. The 21st century is witnessing a new round of these debates in which some of the foundational assumptions of earlier rounds – such as the unique character of religion and the comprehensive sovereignty of the state – are now being contested. Laborde's volume engages with two important new ways of addressing this problematic: the critical religion approach of the Foucauldian-Assadian school, and the liberal egalitarian approach of the neo-Rawlsians.[1] She lucidly identifies the 'critical religion' challenge to secularism and to liberalism, and cogently analyzes the various liberal egalitarian responses. While her own approach is a version of liberal egalitarianism, it takes seriously the critical religion challenge more than most liberals do while improving upon and offering a distinctive version of the egalitarian approach. Her alternative engages with the ethical, epistemic and legal-political theoretical versions of the latter, with the aim of delivering a universal normative theory of minimal secularism – i.e. one that is intrinsic to political egalitarian liberalism. Indeed her core intuition, which I share, is that liberal-egalitarian democratic ideals are not restricted to their western historical context of emergence but, if properly construed, have trans-cultural value (pp. 26–30 and pp. 113–159).[2] Genesis, she rightly argues, is not identical to justification and thus the mere fact that certain norms, principles or even institutions emerged in a particular context or epoch does not make them irredeemably particular. Nor is their emergence elsewhere invariably a sign of illegitimate colonial imposition. What matters is their justification not their genesis. With this basic move, Laborde puts to rest much of the critical religionists' critique of liberalism insofar as they tend to conflate the philosophical and justificatory levels with historical forms and patterns of emergence.

Indeed I think the point must be also made regarding social structure. Liberal democracy and the political or minimal secularism it presupposes has structural presuppositions – differentiation among the spheres of society – and it is this that opens up the question of how the differentiated domains do or should interrelate: the quintessential question regarding religion and the state (Cohen, 2015, 2016). Differentiation is not identical to strict separation or 'no' relation between the political and the religious. We all know the stories about secularization, differentiation, the emergence of the modern sovereign state in the West, the 'Westphalian' version of establishment, and the contentious state-religion relations all this triggered. But genesis is not identical to structure. The power constellations, struggles, strategies and projects surrounding the genesis of the modern state do not 'reveal' its structure or logic: these require a distinct analysis. Nor do they show that the sovereign state is irrevocably western, Christian or secular, its Western genesis and its imposition elsewhere through colonial, imperial and then post-colonial developments notwithstanding. I have in my own writings following Bhargava, constructed an ideal type of 'political secularism' that is close to Laborde's idea of minimal secularism, insofar as both assume structural differentiation, focus on appropriate modes of interrelation of the state and religion, as well as issues of normative justification from a liberal democratic perspective.[3] I too am convinced that political or minimal secularism is intrinsic to liberal constitutional democracy albeit as a necessary though hardly a sufficient condition.

These analytic distinctions are central to the Laborde's approach to religion-state relations, namely, normative political theory. Her question is not whether secularism or the separation of state, politics and religion is intrinsically liberal, the obvious examples of myriad authoritarian secular political regimes is ample proof to the contrary. Rather the question is whether a philosophically defensible normative ideal of liberal democracy must be secular and in what way (pp. 113–159). Because the critical religionists reject normative political theory in general and liberalism in particular, construing both as part and parcel of modern (and contemporary) forms of governmentality – strategies of power to produce and govern docile bodies and souls–the very question animating Laborde's work is ruled out as either naive or disingenuous. But as Laborde cleverly shows, the critical religionists' approach, insofar as it is critical, relies on normative commitments about which it is not forthcoming and typically fails to offer an alternative to the institutional forms and political relations it genealogically uncovers and critiques. The prime example is the analysis of the sovereign state, as perforce western, secularizing, and arbitrarily interventionist regarding, and even producing the very category of religion in its liberal or illiberal variants.[4] Laborde nicely pinpoints the core difference in methodological approaches: Foucauldian critical religionists construe secularization – the shift of areas traditionally regulated by religious authorities and norms into the ambit of the state – as a new mode of governmentality that produces subjects, and religion itself as objects of regulation toward which the state, whatever its political regime, cannot be neutral. From the perspective of normative, liberal-democratic theory, these developments, and the regulation of domains including the family, education, health, welfare, sexuality by the civil law – means that they are now sites for the pursuit of interpersonal liberal justice (p. 108). But the normative liberal reading does not imply that empirical or historical state policies are progressive, impartial or neutral per se: rather the point is that education, family, sexuality, gender relations are no longer immune from the constitutional principles of personal freedom, and equal liberty for all (Cohen 2002). While each of these approaches perforce screen out the concerns of the other, Laborde's text shows that one must be reflective about this and see that each can play an important analytic role. I concur that normative philosophical analysis has the advantage that it can make its normative commitments clear and has no hesitation in proposing political alternatives, while the critical religionists, as good Foucauldians, are unable or unwilling to do so for this would entail abandoning their methodological orientation.

This comment focuses on an issue also raised by a third approach to religion and the state that Laborde also engages with which she labels, following Schwartzman and Schragger, 'religious institutionalism' (Schragger & Schwartzman, 2016). In my own work I have referred to it alternatively as 'religious integralism' and 'jurisdictional political pluralism' (Cohen, 2017a). At issue is state sovereignty, and the two distinct levels on which it is engaged by religious institutionalists (and by critical religionists). The first pertains to where and how the state draws the line between the autonomy, the self-governing prerogatives of religious nomos communities and their regulation by the civil law; the second pertains to the prerogative of the state to do the relevant line drawing. The first is about questions of justice and accommodation and the line between the right and the good. Laborde addresses this through her disaggregation method and her theory of minimal secularism as required by liberal principles. The second is about jurisdiction and sovereignty: issues of legitimacy, supremacy and meta-jurisdictional prerogatives ascribed to the state as the supreme and authoritative instance that does the line drawing and determines the competences of all other associations on its territory.

I briefly address both issues and raise some questions regarding Laborde's approach to each.

Minimal secularism and liberalism: matters of justice

Defining minimal secularism is part of identifying the core criteria for a state to qualify as liberal with respect to the regulation of religion. Laborde applies her 'disaggregation strategy' to the concept of religion and to the different liberal values minimal secularism helps sustain, so as to articulate a universal minimal secularism that meets liberal desiderata. Her analysis of the three normative criteria of minimal secularism regarding what she calls the *justifiable*, the *limited* and the *inclusive* state each pertain to a distinct feature of a disaggregated concept/assessment of religion: religion as *non-accessible*, religion as *comprehensive* and religion as *divisive* (pp. 113–159). In making these distinctions, Laborde clarifies what on her view violates liberal legitimacy and the minimal secularism it requires. She argues that liberal legitimacy requires that reasons given by state officials to justify law and public policy must be accessible; practices of recognition and rights distribution must be non-divisive; and equal personal liberty must be guaranteed. Accordingly, those features of religion (or non-religious analogues) that are non-accessible, divisive, or comprehensive must not be accommodated, invoked or institutionalized by the state if it is to meet the basic requirements of liberal legitimacy (pp. 113–159). I quite agree with Laborde that accessibility of justificatory reasons for laws and policies is the correct criterion and that liberals must defend liberalism in substantive terms as the morally correct theory (that insists on the equal liberty and equal status of every individual). I also agree that philosophical liberalism itself provides the necessary normative criteria for inclusiveness in and limits on the liberal state.

Regarding the idea of the limited state and the issue of comprehensiveness, the liberal principle is that practices pertaining to personal ethics should not be coercively enforced on individuals. Liberal minimal secularism entails that the state does not intrusively regulate the ethics of the self (Foucault) or violate what Dworkin called individual ethical integrity and independence.[5] Liberalism is weakly perfectionist, rooted in a thin conception of the good and the ethically salient freedom it protects is the individual's freedom to live by her own conception of ethics…with appropriate provisos regarding harms to and the rights of others (pp. 144–145). Accordingly, liberalism provides internal limits to the civil polity, in the form of negative liberties and basic rights, in tune with the principles of equal liberty and equal concern and respect for all individuals. The egalitarian liberalism Laborde supports merges civil (non-perfectionist) republicanism with political liberalism: such that rights and obligations follow from what is entailed by participating in a fair system of cooperation by those with different worldviews, conceptions of the good or religions. On this hybrid approach, there is no baseline of maximal pre-political freedom against which each law must be justified in relation to a compelling state interest (the liberal-libertarian view). Neither is there a pro tanto freedom to practice religion without regard for the overall framework in which peoples' opportunities are fairly structured. On the liberal egalitarian-civil republican view, the civil polity provides a fair framework for sharing the benefits and burdens of a common life and thus legitimately regulates the exercise of the rights and liberties accordingly. Indeed.

However, I have some reservations regarding the way Laborde parses the issue of divisiveness and inclusion. The liberal principles at issue are civic equality, inclusiveness and equality of treatment. The relevant feature of religion Laborde highlights is whether it is divisive or not. Laborde leaves aside the 'easy question' of unequal rights arguing that no constitutional theocracy or 'religious democracy' that fails to grant equal rights to minority citizens meets basic criteria of liberal legitimacy (p. 132). She focuses instead on the tricky question of state endorsements in the form of symbolic establishments that tend to make religious identity a part of civic identity and the problems of exclusion and expressive inequality this raises. She is right that this is an analytically distinct concern from issues of distributive justice. It is tricky because not all endorsements are discriminatory, some are benign, and the task is to develop criteria for distinguishing among them. Laborde suggests that symbolic religious establishment is problematic when it tightly associates state citizenship with a collective religious identity that is politically divisive in an unreasonable and intractable way (pp. 135–136). Divisiveness is key: insofar as the state associates itself closely with the symbols of a particular religious identity it turns adherents of other religions or religious identities, recognized or not, into minorities and symbolically at least, into second-class citizens. If a religious identity is part of a deep fault line of social and political division the state should not endorse its symbols or establish it in any way. Indeed doing so constructs and/or politicizes religious difference. Yet the majority of the world's people live under regimes that are what Hirschl calls constitutional theocracies – where a religion is formally enshrined in the state or where religious affiliation is a pillar of collective political identity.[6] Laborde's concern, in part, is to show that her model of minimal secularism can pertain to some of these regimes *and*, pace Hirschl, that one should not label all regimes that do not separate religion and the state as theocratic or as perforce illiberal (p. 151).

This intuition fits with my own efforts to articulate an ideal type of political secularism that would allow us to place different regimes on a spectrum, the two ends of which are theocracy and coercive establishment (Cohen, 2016). By 'theocracy' I mean a system in which the ultimate political decision-making power is in the hands of clerics; by 'coercive establishment,' I mean that political elites rather than clerics rule and establish one religion as true, as a constituent part of national identity (who we are), and enforce adherence to what it deems appropriate religious practice and doctrines, while excluding or punishing practitioners of other religions. Between the two extremes is a wide range of more or less legitimate state religion relations from a liberal perspective. There is indeed no single regime of separation or interrelation that is required by liberalism (or democracy). Yet I don't find the way Laborde deploys her criterion of political divisiveness to be fully convincing.

Laborde argues that a liberal democratic state cannot define itself as Hindu, Jewish or Muslim in contexts where such identities have become deep fault lines of political division, as in India, Israel, Egypt. She is also aware that so-called 'religious differences' are often created and instrumentalized by the state (p. 137). She knows that religious identities can function as markers of social vulnerability, exclusion and domination and that symbolic establishment can render religious identities salient in ways that affirm and consolidate boundaries between dominant and dominated groups. The wrong of official endorsement of the majority religion is indeed that it makes minority status relevant, negatively, to civic status (p. 137). And it matters whether state-endorsed symbols are politically divisive. But *all* religious identities are divisive if politicized and made part of the identity of the polity, for those who do not belong and even possibly for those who do, yet don't practice, or who disagree with the state's use of religious symbols, or who oppose state symbolic appropriation and/or codification of religion as tantamount to cooptation and corruption of the religious quality of norms and practices. This would apply to 'Divinitia' an ideal type constructed by Laborde in her text, insofar as the state symbolically recognizes one religion albeit not in a way that infringes on the equal citizenship of non-adherents (p. 151). Laborde argues that Divinitia is compatible with her understanding of minimal secularism and with liberal legitimacy. But this seems to undercut her position on symbolic establishment, which stresses inclusiveness because it perforce renders religion a salient mode of sociopolitical belonging. When a state identifies with a religion, when it enshrines it as 'a' or 'the' source of law in its constitution (hoping to sacralise the constitution itself), when it enforces what it takes to be its tenets in its courts for church members or allows religious courts to do the enforcing regarding certain domains (typically family law and education), even if it does not breach the accessibility condition or personal liberty directly and accords equivalent rights to other religious groups, it nonetheless privileges one religion and lays the groundwork for inequality, exclusions, resentments, divisiveness and for inflammatory identity politics. Indeed, if these sorts of symbolic establishment are not divisive at time 1, politically endorsing a majority religion invites divisiveness down the line at time 2, by rendering religious identity politically salient, by inviting the wrong kind of majoritarian politics: i.e. quasi-racialized, substantive conceptions of religious belonging blurred with civic identity and law making on that basis – and by implicitly casting even legally recognized minority religions as other, and inferior. Given path dependence and a particular constellation of forces, many states that in the past endorsed a particular religion continue to establish it symbolically, under the premise that the endorsements are now benign and establishment, vestigial. But state endorsement of religion is never innocent and stands as an open invitation to exclusionary religious nationalism.

Pragmatically it may not be appropriate to take down long-standing religious symbols from say, public buildings and lands especially if no one is objecting to them, or to undo other endorsements of religion or religions in a given constellation. But it is important not to underestimate the power of the symbolic, especially of religious symbols as markers of identity, inclusion and exclusion. Indeed, one has to ask what work the terms, 'Christian,' 'Hindu,' 'Jewish,' 'Muslim' are doing in the labels: Christian democracy, Jewish democracy, Muslim democracy, Hindu democracy or Christian state, Hindu state, Jewish state, Muslim state? I fear that symbolic endorsement of this sort is inevitably divisive insofar as it invites the construal of other religious and non-religious people as so substantively different than the national religious majority that they could never really become 'one of us' or belong – something quite different then, say, shifting political ideological majorities made up of cross-cutting and shifting alliances.

I realize, of course, that Laborde does not propose or advocate symbolic establishment. Moreover, she and I probably agree that there is no point in insisting on the abolition of all extant forms of state symbolic establishments of religion, if they are not deemed divisive at this time. This is a pragmatic issue: it may be more divisive to undo old symbolic establishments like religious monuments on public land, or Sunday closing laws, especially if no one objects to them and provisions are made for religious minorities to celebrate their own holidays (pp. 148–149). In a secularizing society, they may be considered vestigial and benign historical artifacts. But I would argue strongly against any new symbolic establishments, and against inscribing a religion in the constitution as a source of law or as a part of the national identity of a polity. I also caution against defending old symbolic establishments as normatively unproblematic, like large crosses in the public square, or at the entrance to a town, or Court, once a minority religious group indicates that their presence turns them into second-class citizens. Such symbolic establishments are always available for mobilizations in the form of 'restorative' religious populists who invokes them as proof that non-adherents are really, ultimately 'other' and to demand that 'we' 'take our country back' from alien groups and the elites coddling them, even in quite secular societies. In short, divisiveness is a helpful criterion for distinguishing between benign and discriminatory forms of state recognition of religion but I argue that symbolic establishment and recognition that privileges one religion as the national religion is necessarily divisive. This inevitably will run afoul of Laborde's inclusiveness principle.

Now I am aware that Laborde generally prefers equalizing down instead of equalizing up when it comes to 'vestigial,' allegedly benign establishments such as Anglicanism in Great Britain or Protestantism in Denmark (p. 231). The old compromises and arrangements are strained when new religious groups enter the arena and I quite agree with the anti-corporatist, anti-multiple establishment approach. I think that dis-establishment is better than multiple-establishment from a liberal egalitarian point of view because there are always some religious groups left out of the corporate recognition structure. Moreover, the regulation of religious self-regulation fits perfectly well with a disestablishment regime since the latter, in a liberal constitutional democracy, does not entail strict separation but, rather, calls for regulation of self-regulation, in the right way (Cohen, 2012a). Thus regarding symbolic establishment, the point is not that we have to ferret out all path dependent historical endorsements but a. that new ones should be avoided, b. those that are contested as exclusionary should for liberal reasons of inclusiveness and non discrimination, be dropped and c., those that are not defensible from the perspective of democratic justice should be abolished.[7] The path of disestablishment taken by Norway and Sweden in this regard is the right one from a principled egalitarian liberal perspective.

Let me make one last point on minimal secularism and nonestablishment. Laborde is right, the principle of democratic legitimacy explains why citizens accept the imposition of laws that from their point of view seem unjust and it also explains why different states may opt for one or another reasonable conception of justice and be deemed in compliance with basic liberal principles (pp. 151–152). She draws the conclusion that it is as legitimate for countries with secularized majorities to have laws that reflect their preferences as it is for countries with religious majorities to do the same and she takes liberals to task for not conceding this point. On her concept of minimal secularism, state-religion arrangements can permissibly be sensitive to the religious make up of societies without breach of liberal legitimacy. Indeed. But she insists on symmetry: religious citizens must accept the secular state as reasonable and secular citizens must accept the legitimacy of 'liberal religious states' such as 'Divinitia' as we have seen (p. 151). However I don't find the analogy between the two majorities intuitively convincing although the devil is, to be sure, in the details. Like Laborde, my preferred conception of justice is closer to the progressive arrangements of Secularia, Laborde's model for a liberal constitutional democracy (p. 152). Moreover, I prefer that politically secular liberal constitutional democracies do not enshrine the word 'secular' in their constitutions for that can invite a divisive form of religious identity politics – the U.S, Constitution took the right path on that score. Given the assumption that Divinitia would symbolically recognize one religion, ideal-typically in its Constitutional documents, and would proclaim some laws as religiously inspired (typically the established religion being deemed 'a' or 'the' source the law) even if the justification of those laws is accessible and does not infringe on the personal liberty of non-adherents, I think, as already indicated, that danger of linking civil-religious identities is far greater here. I also have my doubts about Divinitia's liberal, minimally secular credentials in light of its the 3rd through 5th features. These include the proviso that the state may have restrictive laws about abortion, euthanasia, and other practices in bio-ethics, and that religious groups enjoy extended rights of collective autonomy in the name of freedom of association (p. 151). These are in my view too broad and vague. Much depends on what the restrictions these are, who decides their limits and conditions, whether or not they violate principles of gender equality, and other anti-discriminatory norms. What kind of restrictive laws about abortion are acceptable, and how do they differ from regulations in Secularia? Since in Secularia there can be very fine tuned regulations, say of second and third term abortion to protect women's health and with respect to fetal viability, one wonders what further restrictions Divinitia could enact that do not trespass on women's rights or treat then as second class citizens. Additionally, one wonders whether under the heading of bioethical practices, Divinitia could legislate or permit restrictions on the availability, say, of contraception to women? What about refusals to acknowledge same sex unions and so forth? Without more specificity it seems likely that such laws would indeed infringe on the personal liberty and basic rights of non-adherents.

In short, I fear the effort to be even handed risks throwing women under the bus because religious arguments about abortion, contraception, and many other practices in bio ethics, typically entail assumptions endorsing gender hierarchy. Without further elaboration, I am not yet convinced by the construction of the two types of polities – Secularia and Divinitia–as both being sufficiently minimally secular and thus compatible with liberal principles that entail the equal status, rights, opportunity and voice of all individuals regardless of gender or sexuality or sexual orientation. Indeed religious groups could enjoy extended rights of collective autonomy in the name of freedom of association in Secularia while they should be subject to antidiscrimination norms at the very least if they receive state funding, tax exemptions, and provide services to the general public. Nor am I convinced that symbolic recognition/establishment of one religion can avoid infringing on the civic standing of the minorities that are, in part, *produced* by such recognition with the unavoidable consequence that they are not really considered full members of the political community.

Sovereignty: matters of jurisdiction and legitimacy

I turn to the second and deeper issue regarding liberal legitimacy – namely its presumption of the sovereignty of the secular state. In her chapter on state sovereignty and freedom of association, Laborde takes up the issue that I myself have spilt much ink over, namely that of sovereignty, jurisdiction and pluralism as it pertains to religious associations.[8] Laborde rightly notes that state sovereignty provides the frame for liberal neutrality and public reason and while it is constrained by liberal principles of justice, it does not derive from them. Put differently, the liberal non-theocratic state concerns itself with interpersonal relations between free and equal persons and hence with matters of justice and not with the private sphere of the good, even though it does not rule out all appeals to the good in politics (p. 150 and Chapter 3). The question of what pertains to the public domain of justice and what pertains to private domain of the good, i.e. of what are deemed to be self regarding matters of personal ethical integrity and what issues or practices involve public interpersonal justice and thus are legitimately regulated by the state is complex, contested, and the lines are hard to draw. Moreover, the boundaries are not stable. As we know, matters formerly deemed private under the doctrine of entity privacy pertaining to 'the family' – that framed relations between husband and wife, child rearing and so forth as matters of personal ethics–are now seen as involving interpersonal relations where grave injustices can occur and which the civil law must regulate. Thus, the relevant line drawing pertains to a different level of analysis than choosing among different conceptions of justice for the public sphere or the basic structure. It entails the key question of which instance gets to do the line drawing and hence to determine what is a matter of public justice and what is not. The meta-jurisdictional question of the competence to decide competences (what German constitutional theorists call *Kompetenz Kompetenz*) and the meta-jurisdictional authority to delimit the scope of jurisdiction and regulate the scope of autonomy enjoyed by the various nomos communities or associations within a particular territory are at the core of the sovereignty problematic.

As I have argued elsewhere, liberal democracy assumes the comprehensive reach of the civil law (internally limited by liberal, constitutionalist and democratic principles) and the authority of the liberal democratic polity to do the line drawing (Cohen, 2017b). The democratic constitutional state has meta-jurisdictional sovereignty, i.e. the competence to determine competences and to impose the supremacy of civil law, including regulation of autonomous self-regulating civil society associations in the territory (Cohen, 2017a, 2017b). But I have also argued that this fundamental presupposition – of liberal justice, democracy, and of political or minimal secularism – is precisely what is being challenged by jurisdictional pluralists, by some religious institutionalists and to some extent also by the critical religionists (along with certain versions of cosmopolitanism, neoliberal economic ideologists, religious fundamentalists and so forth) (Cohen, forthcoming). Thus what has been taken as a given now has to be justified, again. In my own work I foreground this challenge and the jurisdictional sovereignty question as the most ultimate regarding the relation of religious organizations and the state. So of course I think Laborde is right, egalitarian liberals must face the sovereignty question again and provide normative justification for the supremacy of the authority and civil law of the liberal democratic polity over internal contenders.

Laborde and I both argue that democratic procedures are the only fair way to solve disagreements about the scope of religious autonomy and that political or minimal secularism entail the principle of democratic sovereignty. Liberal egalitarianism relies on presumption of the sovereign secular democratic state, the comprehensive scope of the civil law and its role and supremacy in deciding the boundary and scope of religious autonomy (pp. 161–164).[9] Laborde rightly asserts that state sovereignty provides the background condition or frame within which liberal neutrality and consideration of matters of justice first arise and can be adjudicated. Liberalism presupposes this supremacy of the civil and political. Indeed state secularism precedes neutrality historically and logically.

Laborde is also right that neither liberal neutrality nor public reason can provide the normative justification for state sovereignty. In other words, meta-jurisdictional sovereignty – the prerogative to authoritatively determine the respective spheres of the public/political and the religious, does not derive from liberal neutrality. Based on a distinction between legitimacy and justice, which I endorse, Laborde notes that the former pertains to the justification of the territorial state and its sovereignty, while the latter pertains to interpersonal morality and the norms of the basic structure it establishes and regulates. This distinction allows us to see why different states may justifiably opt for distinct but reasonable conceptions of justice. Moreover it is democratic legitimacy that renders a law legitimate even to those who think it is unjust. Indeed Laborde goes so far as to argue that a sovereign state is legitimate only if it pursues a recognizably liberal conception of justice *and* does so democratically. Accordingly state sovereignty must be limited by liberal democratic principles. For her, and for me, democratic legitimacy is at the core of any normative justification of state sovereignty.

Working with this presumption, Laborde bases the normative justification of state sovereignty on two ideas: first, that an authoritative and stable resolution of conflicts of justice require a final ultimate source of sovereignty: if we are not equally subject to a legitimate authority able to authoritatively delimit and enforce our equal rights of freedom, including associational freedom, we remain vulnerable to the arbitrary will of the powerful (p. 161). Second, democratic states represent the interests of individuals qua individuals regardless of their contingent identities, features, and memberships. While they can be members of many groups, 'their *paramount* interests as free and equal citizens must be represented by a universal-membership association' (p. 162). Thus, the democratic polity must have meta-jurisdictional sovereignty over all other associations and the competence to determine their competence. So minimal secularism presupposes the autonomy of human from divine power and is intimately connected to the modern state form (p. 163). The radicalism of liberalism lies in the fact that it assumes the primacy of the political – the democratic polity's prerogative to decisively fix and enforce through state law, the terms of the social contract – and in the primacy of the identity of individuals as citizens over their identity as believers when these conflict. 'Citizenship trumps religious commitment' (p. 163). Secular liberalism, in short, assumes that reasonable individuals have a higher order interest in living under political justice on this earth rather than in living by the word of God – the full truth as they see it' (p. 163).

But as Laborde herself notes this is hardly a trivial assumption (p. 163). Indeed, it is precisely what those whom I call jurisdictional political pluralists, some religious institutionalists and some critical religionists object to. Her focus in this chapter is on the religious institutionalist arguments for 'church autonomy.'[10] Her strategy in rebutting the critique of 'monist' state sovereignty is two-fold. First, she follows me in arguing that the religious institutionalists misconstrue state sovereignty, wrongly arguing that it is absolute and arbitrary even in a liberal democratic polity and mistakenly concluding that the state has no legitimacy or normative claim to trespass on what religious institutions take to be their jurisdictional domain (p. 167, Cohen 2017a). Indeed, we also agree that the conflation by the critical religionists of liberal democratic with authoritarian states by virtue of both being sovereign and secular is normatively misleading and conceptually confused. I argue that such an approach deprives us of the very possibility of distinguishing between theocratic and politically secular states or between the latter and illiberal states that establish and privilege a single religion and oppress its members (Cohen, forthcoming). Finally, we agree that the liberal democratic state's internal sovereignty is limited by liberal democratic principles and thus it does not act *ultra vires* when it regulates religious or other associations accordingly, or when it determines what pertains to public justice, and delimits the scope of autonomy of religious and other associations, so long as it does so democratically in light of a recognizably liberal conception of justice. In short, as Laborde correctly insists, states, not churches, have *Kompetenz-Kompetenz* – the authority to determine their own spheres of competences, as well as those of other institutions: religious associations do not have this meta-jurisdictional competence (p. 165). Churches may not unilaterally determine the rights and duties of their members as citizens or of other citizens (p. 170).

But as already indicated, jurisdictional pluralists, certain religious institutionalists and the critical religionists do not accept these non-trivial assumptions.[11] They do not accept the primacy of the political or what they call monistic sovereignty whether it is liberal democratic or not (Cohen, 2017a, 2017b). They challenge the idea of the priority of the civil citizen role and its obligations over that religious citizen's obligations to their religious commitments, community, and their god. They reject the state's claim to comprehensive and supreme meta-jurisdictional sovereignty as unacceptable state monism. This is why I refer to them as jurisdictional pluralists. Indeed strong jurisdictional political pluralists and some religious institutionalists speak of two equal and conflicting citizen roles involving two conflicting sovereigns and communities: the civil and the religious (McConnell, 2000; Smith, 2016). Muniz-Fraticelli insists on 'external' limits to state sovereignty posed by independent religious associations, and together with Abner Greene and others, consistently rejects its 'monist' claims, while Steven Smith does quite a lot to resurrect the two-world view and legal pluralism concerning the fundamental autonomy of religious and secular power, also advancing the claim that there is no exclusive sovereignty of the state (Muniz-Fraticelli 2014; Greene, 2012).[12] On these jurisdictional pluralist versions of religious institutionalism, the civil law of the state has no comprehensive reach, public power has no primacy, and churches (religious associations) share meta-jurisdictional authority with the state.

I have subjected these claims to critical analysis (Cohen, 2017b). Indeed these arguments mesh with the critical religionists' critique of the sovereign secular state's structural privatization of religion insofar as the state claims the political for itself, appropriates substantive jurisdictional/political domains from what formerly was regulated by religious norms and authorities (morals, welfare, family law, sexuality, education) and reduces the religious domain to a narrow range of concerns which are still not immune to state oversight (Mahmood, 2016). It is precisely what they call state secularism – the meta-prerogative of the state to draw jurisdictional and competence lines – that they deem unacceptable (*ultra vires*) (p. 166). While they are coy about the institutional and normative implications of their critique, the critical religionists' objection to the public/private distinction, to secularization and to the alleged relegation of religion to the private sphere and/or its reduction to a conception of the good seems to imply either an integralist or a jurisdictional pluralist alternative. They and the religionist institutionalists I mentioned above both challenge the idea that the secular state provides a fair framework for the coexistence of religious and non-religious citizens, regardless of whether it is minimally or politically secular or liberal-democratic. The hegemony and legitimacy of the sovereign secular state is challenged, not accepted. The disagreements are not about different conceptions of justice the state should institutionalize or where it should draw the line between the right and the good. Rather they are foundational in Quong's sense – they seem to go all the way down to the most basic assumptions about forms of life (religious/tribal/communal vs. civil, individualist, associational), societal structure (segmental pluralism vs. cross cutting cleavages), sources of legitimacy (theological vs. democratic), and ultimate sources of law (religious texts or we the people) (Quong, 2011, pp. 204–212). They do not, in short, accept the premise or frame within which different conceptions of justice can emerge and be contested: their disagreement pertains to legitimacy, not simply to conceptions of justice, and to the very distinction between the right and the good, private and public, state and religion. There may be no common ground or shared reasons to resort to, if it is the hegemonic idea of the democratic sovereign and the egalitarian liberal premises this entails, that is being challenged.

Enter Laborde's second strategy: that of deflation. Here she follows the path developed by Schwartzman and Schragger (regarding Supreme Court decisions) in interpreting jurisdictional autonomy talk by the religious institutionalists as rhetorical – as a device to emphasize the normative force of rightful claims on behalf of churches and the religious to accommodation within and by, not over and against, the liberal democratic state (Schragger & Schwartzman, 2016). She cites those (few) passages in the work of Steven Smith and Muniz-Fraticelli where they seem to concede that the claims to jurisdiction they have articulated, can be rephrased in the liberal language of rights (Chapter 5). Accordingly, the 'live question' is not who defers but whether to defer; the state must 'internalize' the external limit imposed by the existence of a competing authority, although it need not defer to reasons of persons qua members of association over reasons qua citizens. The idea is to reinterpret legitimacy and jurisdictional questions back into conflicts about conceptions of liberal justice and to move us onto the issues involved in the bulk of accommodation cases facing courts in liberal democracies. I understand and sympathize with this move.

Indeed Laborde refers to my critique of the efforts of the religious institutionalists (jurisdictional pluralists) to frame accommodation demands in terms of questions of jurisdiction rather than justice, and asserts her preference for replacing religious institutionalists talk of lack of jurisdiction with talk about injustice of state interference when it comes to, say appointment of clergy or determination of religious doctrine (note 2 p. 293, and pp. 169–170). The difference is that for the former any interference is pro tanto suspect and illegitimate (*ultra vires*) while for Laborde, beyond gross violations of human rights (including freedom of association) there can be reasonable disagreement about the justice of state intervention. Most cases discussed by the religious institutionalists concern justice in this sense not legitimacy or jurisdiction. I too reject the jurisdictional claims of the religionists. I too reject their translation of matters of justice into jurisdictional questions and I too reject the presumption of a domain of liberty prior to and outside of the civil polity and beyond the scope of civil law. But those who are serious about making jurisdictional claims ultimately reject, despite recent disclaimers, the translation of what they see as religious questions into matters of liberal justice for the sovereign state to decide. Indeed, we know the key areas over which the contestation occurs: family law, gender relations, education, sexuality – and it is precisely secularization in the sense of the large scale transfer of coercive power from the church and divinely appointed authorities to the sovereign civil state regarding these, that is at issue. Whether something is a matter of justice or jurisdiction in short is what is being contested by religious jurisdictional pluralists and theocrats and the point is to make state sovereignty appear as *ultra vires* when it regulates religious associations or matters of family law, sexuality, education in ways that conflict with religious dogma, or commitments.

So, I am uneasy with Laborde's rather quick dismissal of the jurisdictional challenge. After all, the bulk of the talk of the pluralists and some key religious institutionalists is about jurisdiction, and their invocation of legal and political pluralism, their critiques of state sovereignty, their denial of its comprehensive scope, their resurrection of medieval models of plural sovereignty and their talk of another, higher sovereign to whom the religious individual and the state owes deference and whose domain is an 'external' limit to the state, is pervasive in their writings, and hardly a mere rhetorical flourish. In today's context it is also quite dangerous. Challenges to state sovereignty and to the regulatory reach, primacy and authority of public civil institutions and civil law on every level, national regional and supranational, are proliferating. These challenges come from global finance, neoliberal transnational corporate economic actors and from the politicized corporate religious actors. Liberal democracy everywhere is under siege: not only the flawed empirical institutional arrangements in each country but also the fundamental normative principles as well. We cannot assume that achievements on the normative and institutional level of constitutional democracies aren't threatened. They are. The stakes of the struggle are the identification of which areas of social life are justice-apt, who decides this meta-jurisdictional question, and not only which theory of justice is the best one within a clearly hegemonic liberal democratic politically secular polity. So I take the revival of jurisdictional political pluralist discourse by some prominent religious institutionalists very seriously indeed. This is not to deny that there are religious institutionalists like Douglas Laycock, who argue for church autonomy and the ministerial exception without making a jurisdictional pluralist claim, but as a matter of justice. Nevertheless, I think we need more from Laborde on the jurisdictional question because I doubt it will go away and I fear that those who do not accept the core intuition behind the notion of liberal democratic state sovereignty (the primacy of civil law) are quite serious about their projects. Indeed, too many insist that the issue of 'church autonomy' cannot be treated as a matter of associational freedom, but rather regard it as unique, involving deeper issues the prerogatives of ordinary voluntary associations.

That said, Laborde is right to try to devise a liberal theory of associational freedom to address those accommodation/exemption issues that can be handled within the liberal democratic frame. She applies her disaggregating 'interpretive approach' to the general puzzle of collective religious exemptions, identifying two key interests or criteria that independently may justify exemptions and when they come together, special treatment for religious groups. In tune with her egalitarian-liberal orientation and interpretive approach, she does not treat religious associations as unique. Rather she notes that all voluntary associations have a strong interest in *coherence* (the ability to live by their own standards, purposes and commitments) and of some of them, have a special claim to special *competence* (to interpret their own standards, purposes and commitments). I have only a few minor points to make here.

Laborde rightly rejects the now dominant approach in the U.S. that has constitutionalized 'the ministerial exception' for churches, according them immunity to an ever widening array of anti-discrimination labor laws and shielding them from legal scrutiny in the employment of those it labels ministers (p. 177). I concur with the thrust of her method of disaggregation aimed at specifying the values and interests at stake. But I am uneasy with the coherence idea for the following reasons. First, it is difficult to apply. As we know, the core and periphery of religious doctrine changes over time. Coherence interests refer to the association's members' ability to live by their group's standards, purposes and commitments – they entail ethical integrity on the level of the group. But there can be disagreements within a religious group regarding which elements of doctrine and practice are central or peripheral to the group's core religious identity. Such disputes raise questions regarding which sub group of members is the appropriate one to determine the kinds of coherence interests the group has. It may be nearly impossible to identify precisely the ethos of large diverse religions such as 'Judaism' or 'Christianity' or 'Islam'; indeed these are frequently, if not always contested. If male privilege in kinship relations, marriage, inheritance, divorce, child custody is deemed central to the coherence of say Islam, or Orthodox Judaism, or fundamentalist Christianity, and to the solidarity that constitutes the religious community, should the state defer?

I understand that Laborde sees coherence interests as providing a pro tanto claim for accommodation and that exemptions should be denied if there are weightier countervailing reasons. She does not deem the criterion of coherence to be a sufficient condition for granting exemptions. India after it achieved independence provides a compelling example of weighty countervailing reasons: the fact that caste restrictions regarding untouchables in the temples were deemed to be core doctrine of Hinduism, did not deter the liberal social democratic state from developing policies geared toward ending these injustices and indeed challenging caste based rules of labor and interaction altogether. Certainly, Laborde would not hesitate in supporting these policies and would not endorse exemptions to equality principles in such a case. Interestingly, today, the alleged centrality of caste to Hinduism is now being contested by historians, and by political theorists (Dirks, 2001; Mantena, 2010). So coherence is, as indicated, hard to pin down as is the centrality or peripheral nature of actions or practices to the ethical requirements of a religion.

It is important to note that Laborde's argument about the moral force of exemption claims does not reside in their compatibility with communal traditions or in the goal of maintaining coherence with the groups' ethical commitments and actions. Rather the moral force lies in their importance to individual ethical integrity and the value the individual herself gives to communal membership (p. 213). I accept that individual ethical integrity is an important ideal for everyone not only for the religious, and being forced to violate it by the State without good reasons is an injustice. But one person's ethical integrity may entail another's subordination. With respect to the freedom of association, and the ethical integrity at issue of adherents, the idea is that endorsement by the individual member of the association's proclaimed ethical norms is indeed 'free.' The presumption is that membership in and endorsement of the group's values is voluntary. But, given that socialization into religion is typically primary socialization and thus involuntary – i.e. membership is ascribed (by parents) to children and exit for adults can thus very hard (costing community and family belonging), given that e.g. gender injustice is learned at an early age and tends to bleed into other domains if it has religious sanction, I have doubts about the coherence principle with regard to such issues. I ask whether religious groups can really be treated as voluntary associations like others and I wonder whether, at the very least, we should withhold state support from religious institutions that perpetuate invidious gender discrimination – I have in mind tax exemptions and other privileges, if we take gender justice seriously. The state should not be made complicit with group norms that breach liberal principles of equality and non-discrimination even if it permits such groups to exist. To be sure this stand depends, in Laborde's theory, on whether we deem assertions about and practices that entail the subordination of women to be morally abhorrent or merely morally ambivalent (pp. 214–217).[13]

Whatever the answer, Laborde's excellent book and especially her disaggregation strategy puts us on the right path and calls upon us to follow her lead and reflect seriously and cogently on these issues.

Notes

1. In the first group, among others, are Asad (2003), Cavanaugh (2009), Danchin (2011; 2015), Hurd (2015) and Mahmood (2005; 2016). The neo-Rawlsian egalitarian liberals include, among others, Eisgruber and Sager (2007) and Dworkin (2013).
2. Unless otherwise specified, all page references are to Laborde (2017).
3. Cohen (2016). I prefer the term political secularism because it evokes political liberalism yet doesn't entail that society must be irreligious just because the state is.

4. For my critique of this, see Cohen (forthcoming).
5. Dworkin (2013). See the discussion in Laborde (pp. 44–82 and 145–146).
6. Hirschl (2010). Hirschl does not adequately distinguish between theocracy and establishment, in my view. See Below.
7. We are quite close on this issue (p. 231).
8. For an early attempt see Cohen (2012a).
9. Political liberalism can also secured in a federation. Just what sovereignty regime is entailed for the public power in a state or federal polity depends on the sovereignty regime in place in the international community. Comprehensiveness of civil law need not mean exclusivity, e.g. in Europe, European law also has efficacy within each sovereign state. I speak of the state because that is the context in which religion: state issues arise but of course they arise in no state federations as well as e.g. in the EU. On this see Cohen (2012b).
10. For her discussion of the ambiguities in the critical religion theorists' 'debunking' of the sovereign line drawing prerogative see p. 166 where she points out that it is unclear whether the believe states draw the line unjustly or undemocratically or whether they have no pro tanto legitimacy to do so in the first place or to define what is a harm, or fair opportunity and so on.
11. I place Victor Muniz-Fracticelli (2014) and Abner S. Greene (2012) in the category of strong jurisdictional pluralists who challenge these assumptions. Steven D. Smith (2010) and Michel McConnell (2000) are among the religious institutionalists who challenge these assumptions as well.. Others like David Laycock and Christopher Lund have been much more circumspect, arguing for church autonomy and the ministerial exception as a matter of justice not of sovereignty. They do not challenge the sovereignty of the state.
12. See my discussion: Cohen (2017a).
13. I deem the subordination of women to be morally abhorrent and there should be no state complicity with it.

Disclosure statement

No potential conflict of interest was reported by the author.

References

Asad, T. (2003). *Formations of the secular*. Stanford University Press, Stanford, Califoria.

Cavanaugh, W. (2009). *The myth of religious violence*. Oxford University Press,Oxford, Great Britain

Cohen, J. L. (2002). *Regulating intimacy*. Princeton, New Jersey: Princeton University Press.

Cohen, J. L. (2012a). The politics and risks of the new legal pluralism in the domain of intimacy. *ICON, 10*(2), 380–397.

Cohen, J. L. (2012b). *Globalization and sovereignty*. Cambridge University Press, Cambridge, Great Britain

Cohen, J. L. (2016). Rethinking political secularism and the american model of constitutional dualism. In J. L. Cohen & C. Laborde (Eds.), *Religion, secularism and constitutional democracy* (pp. 113–156). Columbia University Press, New York, USA

Cohen, J. L. (2017a). Sovereignty, the corporate religious and jurisdictional political pluralism. In C. Laborde & A. Bardon (Eds.), *Religion in liberal political philosophy* (pp. 83–102). Oxford: Oxford University Press.

Cohen, J. L., forthcoming. On the genealogy and legitimacy of the politically secular state. *Constellations*. retrieved from https://ssrn.com/abstract=2874535.

Cohen, J.L., 2015. Freedom of religion, Inc. *Netherlands Journal of Legal Philosophy* 44 (3),169–211.

Cohen, J.L., 2017b. Sovereignty, the corporate religious and jurisdictional political pluralism. *Theoretical Inquiries in Law* 18(2),547–575.

Danchin, P. (2011). Islam in the secular nomos of the European court of human rights. *Michigan Journal of International Law*, 32, 240-252

Danchin, P., et al (2015). Religious freedom in the panopticon of enlightenment rationality. In W. F. Sullivan, Elizabeth Shakman Hurd, Saba Mahmood, Peter G. Danchin, (Eds), *Politics of religious freedom*. The University of Chicago Press. Chicago, Illinois

Dirks, D. (2001). *Castes of mind*. Princeton University Press. Princeton, New Jersey

Dworkin, R. (2013). *Religion without god*. Harvard University Press.Cambridge, Massachusetts

Eisgruber, C., & Sager, L. (2007). *Religious freedom and the constitution*. Harvard University Press.Cambridge, Massachusetts

Greene, A. (2012). *Against obligation*. Harvard University Press.Cambridge, Massachusetts

Hirschl, R. (2010). *Constitutional theocracy*. Harvard University Press.Cambridge, Massachusett

Hurd, E. S. (2015). *Beyond religious freedom*. Princeton University Press.PrincetonNew Jersey

Laborde, C. (2017). *Liberalism's Religion*. Harvard University Press. Cambridge, Massachusetts

Mahmood, S. (2005). *The politics of piety*. Princeton University Press. Princeton, New Jersey

Mahmood, S. (2016). *Religious difference in a secular age*. Princeton University Press.

Mantena, K. (2010). *Alibis of empire*. Princeton University Press. Princeton, New Jersey

McConnell, M. (2000). Believers as equal citizens. In N. L. Rosenblum (Ed.), *Obligations of citizenship and the demands of faith* (pp. 90–110). Princeton University Press. Princeton, New Jersey

Muñiz-Fraticelli, V. (2014). *The structure of pluralism*. Oxford University Press.Oxford, Great Britain

Quong, J. (2011). *Liberalism without perfection*. Oxford University Press.Oxford, Great Britain

Schragger, R., & Schwartzman, M. (2016). Some realism about corporate rights. In M. Schwartzman, C. Flanders, & Z. Robinson (Eds), *The Rise of corporate religious liberty* (pp. 345–374). Oxford University Press.Oxford, Great Britain

Smith, S. D. (2010). *The disenchantment of secular discourse*. Harvard University Press. Cambridge, Massachusetts

Smith, S. D. (2016). The jurisdictional conception of church autonomy. In M. Schwartzman, C. Flanders, & Z. Robinson (Eds), *The rise of corporate Religious Liberty* (pp. 19–38). Oxford University Press. Oxford,Great Britain

Liberalism and religion: the plural grounds of separation

Chiara Cordelli

ABSTRACT
In what sense, and to what extent, should a liberal state be secular? Many interpret liberal-egalitarian political theory as dictating a radical separation between church and state. Against this view, Cécile Laborde has powerfully argued that, in fact, liberal-egalitarianism is not committed to strict separation as such. Laborde understands the liberal-egalitarian commitment to separation as ultimately grounded on a principle of neutrality. However, she argues that the conception of neutrality to which liberal egalitarians are committed is much more 'restricted' than it is often thought. If a commitment to separation is derivative from a commitment to neutrality, then, if neutrality is restricted, secularism is minimal. This means that not all forms of religious establishment should be regarded as impermissible from a liberal-egalitarian perspective. Contra Laborde, I argue that restricted neutrality should not be understood as the only ground of separation. Separation has plural grounds. Forms of religious recognition that do not violate any of the requirements of restricted neutrality may still be regarded as impermissible from a liberal-egalitarian perspective, if they (1) violate a basic commitment to fairness, (2) treat citizens in a patronizing way and/or (3) violate, in their justification, a requirement of sincerity, as grounded on reciprocity.

Introduction

In what sense, and to what extent, should a liberal state be secular? Should liberal-egalitarians be committed to a strict separation between state and religion? Or, are certain forms of religious establishment compatible with the liberal-egalitarian project? These are crucial questions that have occupied the minds of political and legal philosophers for a long time. The predominant tendency has been to interpret liberal-egalitarian political thought as dictating a radical separation between religion and politics, church and state (Audi, 1989).

If early modern liberal political thinkers such as John Locke pointed to toleration as the guiding virtue of legitimate political authorities in relation to the treatment of religious minorities, contemporary political liberals have shifted their focus from toleration to a much more demanding institutional restraint: liberal neutrality (see, e.g. Dworkin, 1985). The liberal state should not simply tolerate religious minorities, for insofar as we can only tolerate what we disapprove mere toleration would effectively entail state disapproval of some particular ways of living. Rather, the liberal state should take a stance of full neutrality between majority and minority religions, as well as between religious and non-religious beliefs and conceptions of the good, at least to the extent that these meet certain minimal standards of reasonableness.

On the one hand, coercive state policies should be justified by appealing to public reasons that do not make essential reference to any particular comprehensive conception of the good life (Quong, 2011). This rules out justifying state action by appealing to religious reasons. On the other hand, the liberal state should be radically anti-perfectionist in the kind of policies it pursues. It should not favour or disfavour, encourage or discourage, one conception of the good over others, thereby passing a judgement on the superiority of certain ways of living over others. It should not be given the discretionary authority 'to choose among sincere convictions to decide which are worthy of special protection and which not' (Dworkin, 2013). This means that, as far as religion is concerned, the liberal state should neither provide special recognition (e.g. in the form of special subsidies or special exemptions) to religious practices and institutions nor should it impose special burdens on the latter. Religion and politics, church and state should be strictly separated. This radical separationist stance, it has long been assumed, is a direct institutional implication of a commitment to liberal neutrality.

However, not all liberal-egalitarians share this view. In a recent, excellent book, *Liberalism's Religion* (2017), Cécile Laborde powerfully argues that, in fact, liberal-egalitarianism is not committed to strict separation as such, and should not be so interpreted. Societies which justify certain policies by appealing to religious reasons and that provide special protection or recognition to religion can still be regarded as legitimate liberal-egalitarian societies, provided that they meet certain conditions. Importantly, Laborde does not reject, indeed she fully endorses, the view that liberals' commitment to the separation between state and religion is a direct, institutional implication of a broader principle of neutrality. Yet, through a critical reading and insightful analysis of major contemporary liberal egalitarian thinkers, she shows that the conception of neutrality liberal egalitarians are, in fact, committed to is much more 'restricted' than it is often thought (p. 71). If a commitment to separation is derivative from a commitment to neutrality, then, Laborde concludes that 'Just as neutrality is restricted, so secularism is minimal' (p. 116).

But what does it mean for secularism to be minimal? In Laborde's view (p. 150), this means that forms of religious or cultural establishment are impermissible and incompatible with liberal-egalitarian legitimacy, if and only if, they violate at least one of the following three principles:

(1) When a practice relates to comprehensive ethics, it should not be coercively enforced on individuals.
(2) When a social identity is a marker of vulnerability and domination, it should not be symbolically endorsed and promoted by the state.
(3) When a reason is not generally accessible, it should not be appealed to by state officials to justify state coercion.[1]

When forms of religious establishment or recognition do not infringe upon any of these principles, they ought to be regarded as compatible with the legitimacy of the liberal-egalitarian state (see Chapter 4).

In this essay, I examine Laborde's argument in support of minimal secularism and open up some critical questions about the scope of the above principles. I argue that these principles under-reach, insofar as there are forms of cultural or religious recognition that do not violate any of the three principles above but should still be regarded as impermissible from a liberal-egalitarian perspective. My critical reading of Laborde's theory of minimal secularism opens up a broader question. The question is whether we ought to regard liberal egalitarians' commitment to separation as an implication or instance of a principle of restricted neutrality alone, or whether we should, to use a concept central to Laborde's work, further 'disaggregate' the values that support such a commitment. On this line of analysis, I will suggest that a basic commitment to fairness has a more central place in grounding separation than Laborde herself acknowledges.

From neutrality to separation

Separation, in Laborde's view, is the institutional implication of a broader principle of liberal neutrality. Through her interpretative reconstruction of contemporary liberal-egalitarianism, Laborde identifies three main grounds of neutrality. According to a first line of thought, which she attributes to Ronald Dworkin, the grounding value of state neutrality is *ethical independence*. Following Dworkin, Laborde defines ethical independence as 'the protected right not to have one's *ethical evaluations* usurped by the state' (p. 145). Importantly, she distinguishes (pp. 73–74) ethical independence from the more expansive personal freedom to pursue whatever preference or conception of the good one happens to have, which we may call 'bare freedom.'

'Ethical evaluations' refer, in Dworkin's (2008, pp. 72–73) own terms, to 'convictions about the importance of human life or of achievement in a human life.' The liberal principle of neutrality, so interpreted, commits the state to a presumption of non-interference with matters of ethical foundation, but not to a presumption of non-interference with individuals' non-ethical preferences, conceptions or commitments, such as, for example, leisure preferences (p. 74). The implication for state action of grounding neutrality on ethical independence rather than bare freedom is the following: the neutral state can rightfully limit people's bare freedom to pursue their projects out of sound reasons, but it should refrain from interfering in ethically salient and integrity-related interests, unless perhaps when there is a compelling state interest for doing so (p. 147). As Laborde (p. 148) explains, 'Although the state should not appeal to the truth of any comprehensive doctrine, even to burden ordinary freedoms, it should take care not unreasonably to burden integrity-related liberties, even in the name of non-comprehensive reasons.'

From this restricted interpretation of liberal neutrality, as grounded on ethical independence rather than bare freedom, Laborde draws the conclusion that while a liberal state must be neutral towards religion when religion is a system of personal ethics (which it often is), it need not be neutral towards religion when it is not. We then arrive to the first principle of minimal secularism: 'when a practice relates to comprehensive ethics, it should not be coercively enforced on individuals' (p. 144). In relation to religious establishment, this means that certain forms of establishment which 'have been genuinely drained of all but ecumenical cultural significance,' such it is the case of the mostly symbolic establishment of the Anglican Church in Great Britain, are compatible with state neutrality (at least in this first sense) for they do not usurp people's ethical judgements and do not infringe on their personal ethics (pp. 152–153). They do no therefore violate the above principle.

But ethical independence is not the only value that, according to Laborde's reconstruction of contemporary liberalism, grounds a commitment to state neutrality. Civic inclusion is a further candidate (p. 137). According to this rationale, neutrality requires that a state avoids endorsing or burdening specific conceptions of the good, including religious ones, when doing so would convey a message of second-class citizenship or disparagement to minorities. Only when practices or conceptions of the good function as 'a marker of social division,' is their endorsement or burdening ruled out by the civic inclusion rationale. We then get to the second principle for limiting forms of permissible establishment or recognition (p. 137): 'When a social identity is a marker of vulnerability and domination, it should not be symbolically endorsed and promoted by the state.' Since some forms of symbolic establishment, such as in the case of the Anglican Church in Great Britain, do not seem to violate this principle, then, Laborde argues that these forms of establishment are compatible with liberal egalitarians' fundamental commitment to state neutrality.

Finally, Laborde (p. 120) identifies a third, epistemic ground for liberal neutrality. People, in her view, can be legitimately coerced in the name of reasons they do not share or agree with, but they cannot be legitimately coerced in the name of reasons that they cannot understand or access. Accessible reasons are fully intelligible but, unlike shared reasons, need not be endorsed according to common standards. Since not all forms of religious establishment are based on inaccessible reasons, we arrive to the third principle for delimiting impermissible forms of establishment (p. 120): 'When a reason is not generally accessible, it should not be appealed to by state officials to justify state coercion.' For instance, to continue with our previous example, the establishment of the Anglican Church can be justified by appealing to reasons, such as the impersonal value of culture or historical continuity, that even if not shared are still accessible and subject to collective evaluation. Therefore, even in this respect, the Anglican establishment is not incompatible with liberal egalitarianism's fundamental commitment to state neutrality.

The conclusion is that liberal egalitarianism does not require strict separation and is compatible with different forms of religious establishment and recognition, as long as they do not infringe upon matters of personal ethics, do not violate civic inclusion and are justified by appeal to accessible reasons.

In the next section, I will express some concerns with Laborde's assumption that we can understand the permissibility (or lack thereof) of certain forms of establishment by simply focusing on restricted neutrality. This is because, I will suggest, considerations of personal ethics, civic inclusion and accessible reasons are not the only reasons why contemporary liberal-egalitarians have endorsed or should endorse a principle of separation between state and religion. I will then argue that the three principles of minimal secularism may not be sufficiently capacious, for they allow for forms of establishment that are incompatible with fundamental liberal-egalitarian commitments.

Beyond neutrality: the plural grounds of separation

It is certainly true that some of the most important contributors to contemporary liberalism, most notably Ronald Dworkin, consider a commitment to neutrality, as based on ethical independence, to be central to their political theory. This commitment is, in many respects, a re-interpretation of modern liberalism's conceptions of toleration. At the same time, however, the liberal-egalitarianism of John Rawls, Dworkin and others distinguishes itself from its modern predecessors in the following fundamental respect: it also gives centrality to questions of *fairness*. If the value of ethical independence is at the core of contemporary liberal-egalitarianism, then fairness is at the core of contemporary liberal-egalitarianism. Therefore, in order to assess the compatibility of certain forms of religious establishment with the liberal-egalitarian project as a whole, one should not only ask whether these forms are compatible with restricted neutrality but also ask whether they are compatible with a basic commitment to fairness.

Most forms of religious establishment or recognition, including symbolic ones, entail some costs. These costs can be marginal, such as the costs of printing religious symbols on the flags of a country, but they can also be more substantial. For example, the establishment of the Anglican Church, albeit mostly symbolic, requires the maintenance of a complex system of ceremonies and procedures, such as those involved in the selection of bishops and archbishops who are considered for appointment by the prime minister and then formally appointed by the monarch. Since the monarch is the Supreme Governor of the Church, the costs of maintaining the system of religious establishment, at least in its current form, cannot be completely separated from the costs of maintaining the monarchy.

If a state funds these costs, whatever their extent, through a public system of taxation that imposes burdens on all citizens, non-religious citizens will be effectively required to subsidize the conceptions of the good of others, while remaining with less resources in their pockets to pursue their own conceptions of the good. This can be regarded, at least *prima facie*, as *unfair* even if the policy of establishment does not, by assumption, violate any of the principles of minimal secularism.

The reason for why this policy could be regarded as unfair is simple. As Rawls (1971, p. 250) puts it, 'there is no more justification for using the state apparatus to compel some citizens to pay for unwanted benefits that others desire than there is to force them to reimburse others for their private expenses.' This seems true even if those who are asked to pay can fully understand and access the reasons for why other citizens want those benefits. After all, I might perfectly understand why you may value a Picasso painting, and I might even be so rich that buying a Picasso painting for you would impose only very modest burdens on me. Nevertheless, you cannot coerce me into buying a Picasso painting for you.

Importantly, one can agree that most policies of establishment are unfair, and still believe that they are neutral, in the restricted sense of the term. For example, one can agree with Laborde that the policy supporting the establishment of the Anglican Church is neutral (in the restricted sense), insofar as its justification is not grounded on comprehensive conceptions of the good and does not usurp anyone from their ability to make judgements about matters of private ethics. One may also agree that the policy is not disparaging in any way. Yet, as long as the policy entails some costs, the policy can be unfair if, and insofar as, it forces some people to use their own resources to subsidize goods (1) they do not want or value and (2) the provision of which is not required to secure background conditions of justice to which others have a justice-based claim.

It is not surprising, then, that there is a long tradition in contemporary liberal-egalitarian thought, running from John Rawls (1971) to Alan Patten (2014), which grounds the state's duty to refrain from promoting certain conceptions of the good over others not, or not only, on a commitment to autonomy, ethical independence and civic inclusion, but rather on a basic distributive principle of fairness.[2] Within this tradition, fairness is often included within the grounds of liberal neutrality itself (or even treated as the only ground, in the case of Patten). Since, however, it is not fully clear what the notion of neutrality really adds to the one of fairness (see Cordelli, 2017), and also to avoid terminological confusion, here I will treat fairness and neutrality as two equally important, yet separate, grounds of separation, and I will use the term neutrality to refer only to Laborde's restricted conception of it.

From a liberal-egalitarian perspective, qua free and equal participants in a scheme of social cooperation, citizens have a prima facie claim to a fair, if not fully equal, share of the social product, including economic resources. What counts as a 'fair share' must be determined according to specific principles of justice. True, the content of these principles may be indeterminate and fair democratic processes may be needed to further specify it. Yet, once background conditions of justice – however democratically interpreted – have been defined and secured, what remains in the citizens' pockets should be regarded as rightfully their own. It is thus their right to spend those resources as they wish. Against this distributive baseline, coercively compelling some citizens to subsidize the provision of discretionary benefits, including whatever good that is not required by justice, and which they do not themselves value, means, effectively, to force them to reimburse the private expenses of others. This in turns entails violating their (post-institutional) right to property. This is the case unless those burdened also endorse (beyond accessing) the reasons in support of the policy in question. For it is only by accepting the justification provided to them that they could be regarded as waiving their right to a part of their rightfully held resources.

This is why, from the perspective of fairness, most forms of cultural recognition and religious establishment, including symbolic religious establishment, can be regarded as impermissible violations of property rights, even if they do not violate ethical independence, they do not generate vulnerable groups of second-class citizens and they are supported by accessible reasons and by an appeal to impersonal (as opposed to comprehensive) reasons and values. Therefore, from the perspective of fairness, symbolic establishment can be impermissible even if it does not violate any of the three principles of minimal secularism.

Things would, of course, be different, if one could prove that a policy of religious establishment or recognition is demanded by justice (e.g. as a means of reparation for historical injustice towards vulnerable religious minorities). In that case, support for the policy would not force people to give away a part of their fair share of resources, but it would rather be required to return to others what is rightfully their own. But it is hard to see how the establishment of the Anglican Church, or similar forms of symbolic recognition, could be justified in this way. Laborde herself would seem to agree on this point. However, she argues that these forms of symbolic establishment can be compatible with the liberal-egalitarian project, even if they are justified on grounds of 'the good' rather than 'the right,' as long as these grounds are not fully comprehensive. My view, instead, is that these forms of establishment may well be compatible with a commitment to restricted neutrality, yet they are impermissible because they are incompatible with an equally basic commitment to fairness.

If I am correct that the liberal-egalitarian commitment to separation has plural grounds, including fairness, then the following fourth principle of 'minimal' secularism should be added to Laborde's list:

(4) Whenever the state endorsement or promotion of a practice or social identity would impose some costs on individuals that they are not required to bear on grounds of justice, the state should not endorse or promote that practice unless (a) those who value and support the practice are willing to shoulder the entire costs of supporting it or (b) there is unanimous agreement that the practice ought to be supported (since in neither these cases would some individuals be compelled to pay for a volume of goods over and above their individual valuations).

But, of course, once we accept this principle of fairness, the range of permissible forms of religious establishment vastly shrinks. I will now turn to consider Laborde's possible responses to my argument.

Justice, legitimacy and the problem of ethical salience

Laborde could object that the argument I developed so far misses the point. Her concern, after all, is with the compatibility of certain forms of religious establishment with a requirement of liberal legitimacy, and not with a full conception of social justice. In this respect, she could say that we may regard the establishment of the Anglican Church as unjust, and yet legitimate. I am not sure whether Laborde would like to take this position. Yet, even if we adopt a distinction between justice and legitimacy, the point remains that it would be seriously wrong, because unjust, for a liberal state (like the UK) to maintain this form of establishment. Further, in order to accept Laborde's response, we would need to know more about where the boundaries between justice and legitimacy rest. After all, we may ask, 'shouldn't a conception of liberal-*egalitarian* legitimacy include a commitment to basic principles of fairness?'

However, Laborde could avoid this question and provide a second response to my argument. She could argue that grounding a commitment to the separation between state and religion on a distributive principle of fairness begs the question as to what we can fairly expect people to support or give up in a liberal-democratic society. Recall that, according to Laborde, the liberal state is permitted (and perhaps even required) to treat ethically salient commitments differently from mere preferences. If this is correct, there might be nothing unfair with a tax that happens to burden people's bare freedoms to pursue their own preferences, if this is necessary to subsidize impersonal cultural goods, including certain forms of religious establishment, that a democratic majority has decided to endorse by appealing to accessible, although not unanimously shared, reasons (assuming that these forms of establishment do not violate any of the principles of minimal secularism).

In order for this response to be compelling, however, it is essential that the distinction between ethically salient matters and mere preferences be sustainable. I have some doubts in this respect, to which I now turn.

I think there is an ambiguity in the way Laborde draws the line between ethically salient commitments and mere preferences. On the one hand, ethically salient commitments are defined (p. 56) according to certain substantive features they possess, such as the fact that they are non-contingent and non-negotiable, they concern intimate decisions about birth and sexuality or relate to questions about the ultimate value of human life, they are deep, they are moral and they are different from mere leisure preferences. On the other hand, ethically salient commitments are defined (p. 148) not by reference to substantive features but rather by appeal to the way in which they are endorsed – they should be reflectively endorsed by individuals as key to their sense of integrity, where integrity is defined as congruence between one's principles and one's actions.

One problem, as I see it, is that these two criteria provide potentially conflicting ways of understanding the scope of personal freedom. According to the substantive criterion, trivial preferences (e.g. video games playing) deserve no special protection, no matter the reason for why the agent engages in them. According to the integrity criterion, by contrast, even the most trivial, negotiable and contingent of all preferences could count as ethically salient if the reason why the individual endorses them is grounded on some ethical comprehensive doctrine. For example, the hedonist philosopher who decides that the enjoyment of fleeting gastronomic desires is what the meaning of life is all about will have a *pro tanto* claim to have her personal liberty to pursue these desires robustly protected, while the unreflective person who just likes eating good food won't. Those who have read and are persuaded by Aynd Rand's work will likely regard their habit of accumulating wealth as an ethically salient matter. Their interest in moneymaking would then ground an at least pro tanto claim to special protection. The unreflective banker with the same interest won't have that same claim. To complicate this even more, there will be cases where, according to the 'internal' integrity-based criterion, which is the dominant one in Laborde's account (p. 148), the personal liberty to pursue trivial preferences will deserve more protection than the personal liberty to engage in what, according to the substantive criterion, qualifies as an ethically salient practice. Other things being equal, the liberty of the committed hedonist philosopher to satisfy his gastronomic preferences will deserve, at least *prima facie*, more protection than the sexual freedom of someone who unreflectively engages in consensual sex just for fun. This unpalatable conclusion is also supported by the fact that, according to Laborde, the test to determine what counts as an integrity-based interest and what counts as a bare preference should be ultimately subjective. This strikes me as an unstable way of drawing the boundaries between mere preferences and ethically salient matters.

But assume that we can find a publicly acceptable criterion to distinguish bare preferences from ethical commitments. The fact remains that a liberal state that burdens the self-determination of some in order to provide goods that they do not value (and that are not required by justice) acts in a problematic way, even if no one's ethical independence is infringed upon.

Suppose that a British citizen, call her Margaret, files a public complaint stating that her government should not use any of her money to subsidize whatever costs are entailed in maintaining the establishment of the Anglican Church. This is not, Margaret explains, because the establishment per se confines her to the status of a second-class citizen or expresses a judgement about the superiority of a certain religion over others. It is rather because she wants to use the money to pursue her leisure preferences (e.g. beer-drinking at the pub) rather than to support the conception of the good of the majority, which she does not happen to share. Government responds that since Margaret's preferences are just 'leisure preferences' and do not amount to ethically salient commitments, then Margaret should bear the burdens that her fellow citizens have collectively decided to impose on her, especially since the latter provided her with accessible and non-comprehensive reasons in justification of the policy in question. Things would be different – the government adds – if Margaret could show that her paying extra taxes in support of the policy imposes a burden on an ethically salient commitment. In this case, the government would not be allowed to burden her freedom in order to satisfy her fellow citizens' collective conception of the good. But going to the pub, by Margaret's own admission, is just a preference.

Should Margaret accept the government's answer? I do not think so, and this is so for several reasons.

First, the policy infringes upon Margaret's (and all those who have unreflective leisure preferences) equal opportunity for *self-determination* (Patten, 2014). Self-determination is broader than ethical independence. It is the freedom to pursue the goals and aims that one happens to have, including those preferences to which one has not given much thought. This freedom – here Laborde and I agree – can certainly be restricted or burdened if necessary to secure background conditions of justice. But once these conditions have been secured, no further burdens are warranted unless an acceptable, rather than merely accessible, justification for these burdens can be provided to those subject to them.

Does this means that a liberal state is never justified in providing support for valuable goods such as culture and the arts, or for cultural forms of religious establishment? Not necessarily. It might still be the case that, due to contingent reasons, such forms of support can be required by justice in some circumstances. Further, it is in principle possible that the citizens of a liberal-democracy could agree in advance, on the basis of an overlapping consensus, that decisions that are beyond the scope of justice, such as whether to fund the arts or not, should be left to democratic decision-making. Antecedent overlapping consensus on this procedural principle could then justify imposing burdens to people with conception of the good X, to support goods that are only valued by people with conception of the good Y. This is because, under these conditions, this policy would be the outcome of a fair democratic procedure, which has been previously endorsed by all, including those with conception of the good X, on grounds they themselves could reasonably accept, whether actually or hypothetically. Yet, in the absence of such a previous agreement, it would be illegitimate to leave these choices to a democratic majority.

But there is a second reason for why Margaret should reject the government's answer. Even if the policy in question is not per se grounded on comprehensive reasons, the distinction between bare preferences and ethically salient commitments upon which the policy and its justification rests expresses the judgement that Margaret's (and all those similarly situated) way of living, unlike the way of living of those with deep ethical commitments, is somehow too superficial to deserve special protection. Note, it is true that Margaret's government does not proclaim that there is just one way to live a good life. But its attitude towards her preference can be (arguably) interpreted as sending the message that there are ways to live a life (e.g. going to the pub) that are certainly permissible but not 'important enough,' compared to others. As a citizen, I would find this message disrespectful and patronizing. Yet the nature of this form of disrespect cannot be fully captured by a requirement of civic inclusion, for beer lovers like Margaret are not socially salient minorities and do not pursue socially divisive commitments. It cannot therefore be ruled out by Laborde's second principle.

Finally, should Margaret be convinced by the government's claim that the policy of establishment is justified to her because it is grounded on accessible and non-comprehensive reasons? Laborde's third principle asserts that state officials should not appeal to reasons that are not generally accessible, when justifying state coercion. Yet, in her view, public reasons need not be shared. Both citizens and the state can legitimately appeal to reasons that are accessible, and a fortiori intelligible, but not shared. Whether this principle is compatible with liberal-egalitarianism, it seems to me, ultimately depends on whether one regards the values of sincerity and reciprocity as central to the liberal-egalitarian project. As Jon Quong (2011, Chapter 9) argues, one of the requirements of public reason – a requirement deriving from a principle of reciprocity – is that citizens must sincerely believe that their proposal can be justified to their fellow citizens. If we offered arguments that we believe others have no good reason to accept, we would fail to respect their status as citizens who are owed justifications. Sincerity thus requires that coercive policies are justified by appeal to shared reasons. Suppose Jeremy believes that he is justified in endorsing a given policy for utilitarian reasons alone, and he knows that because his reasons are non-public, albeit fully accessible, they cannot serve as a justification for Immanuel who instead is a committed Kantian. Additionally, suppose that Jeremy believes that the reasons for why Immanuel regards that same policy as justified is unsound, for that reason derives from the Kantian doctrine that Jeremy rejects. Under such conditions, Jeremy cannot endorse the policy in question without violating the requirement of sincerity, even if both Jeremy and Immanuel converge on it. It is only by making the effort of providing Immanuel with reasons that he ought to be able to accept, from his own perspective – i.e. because they are grounded on shared standards of justice – that Jeremy treats Immanuel as an equal who is owed justification, and vice versa. Of course, one could bite the bullet and abandon the requirement of sincerity, but is this a prize liberal-egalitarians should be willing to pay? If not, Margaret could object to her government that, although its policy of religious establishment is justified on the basis of non-comprehensive and accessible reasons, it is nonetheless impermissible because it violates the requirement of sincerity.

Conclusion

Laborde's careful reconstruction of the liberal principle of neutrality as the foundation of liberal-egalitarians' commitment to separation is both illuminating and powerful. However, I have suggested that restricted neutrality should not be understood as the only ground of separation. It follows that forms of cultural or religious recognition that do not violate any of the requirements of restricted neutrality or the corresponding principles of minimal secularism may still be regarded as impermissible from a liberal-egalitarian perspective, if they (1) violate a basic commitment to fairness; (2) treat citizens in a patronizing way and/or (3) violate, in their justification, a requirement of sincerity, as grounded on reciprocity.

Notes

1. I have changed the order in which the three principles appear but nothing in either Laborde's or my argument hangs on a precise ordering.
2. One may argue that for Rawls, the more fundamental ideal of the separateness of persons grounds both a commitment to ethical independence and a commitment to fairness.

Disclosure statement

No potential conflict of interest was reported by the author.

References

Audi, R. (1989). The separation of church and state and the obligations of citizenship. *Philosophy and Public Affairs, 18*, 259–296.
Cordelli, C. (2017). Neutrality of what? *Critical Review of International Social and Political Philosophy, 20*(1), 36–48.
Dworkin, R. (1985). *A matter of principle*. Cambridge, MA: Harvard University Press.
Dworkin, R. (2008). *Is democracy possible here? Principles for a new public debate*. Princeton, NJ: Princeton University Press.
Dworkin, R. (2013). *Religion without god*. Cambridge, MA: Harvard University Press.
Laborde, C. (2017). *Liberalism's religion*. Cambridge, MA: Harvard University Press.
Patten, A. (2014). *Equal recognition. The moral foundations of minority rights*. Princeton, NJ: Princeton University Press.
Quong, J. (2011). *Liberalism without perfection*. Oxford: Oxford University Press.
Rawls, J. (1971). *A theory of justice*. Cambridge, MA: Harvard University Press.

The integrity of religious believers

Paul Bou-Habib

> **ABSTRACT**
> According to Cécile Laborde, persons with religious commitments that are incidentally burdened by generally applicable laws should, under certain circumstances, be provided with an exemption from those laws. Laborde's justification for this view is that religious commitments are a type of commitment with which a person must comply if she is to maintain her integrity. I argue that Laborde's account is insufficiently demanding in terms of the other-regarding attitudes it expects people to have before they can make claims to exemptions based on their integrity. The reason it is insufficiently demanding is that Laborde's account rests on what I call a 'non-moralised' view of integrity. I raise some criticisms of this view and defend the alternative, 'moralised' view of integrity, according to which the value of a religious person's integrity depends on whether the practice she wishes to perform complies with certain moral constraints.

Cécile Laborde defends the view that persons with religious commitments that are incidentally burdened by generally applicable laws should, under certain circumstances, be provided with an exemption from those laws. For example, Orthodox Jews, who believe they have an obligation not to allow their body to be desecrated, may be entitled, under certain circumstances, to an exemption from a legal requirement to undergo post-mortem autopsies that would apply to other persons in the same circumstances.[1] At the same time, Laborde does not believe that just *any* kind of commitment that is incidentally burdened by laws qualifies for legal exemption. If a committed body-builder doesn't want his body tampered with after his death, he will not, presumably, be exempt from an autopsy requirement that would typically apply in his kind of circumstance.[2] The question that naturally arises is why committed body-builders shouldn't get the same treatment as Orthodox Jews. What's so special about a religious commitment?

The answer, according to Laborde, is that religious commitments are a type of commitment with which a person must comply if he is to maintain his integrity. When Orthodox Jews wish not to be subjected to an autopsy after their death, they wish for something in which their integrity is at stake. This isn't true for body-builders as well. Why not? Because integrity requires that an individual 'live in accordance with how she thinks she ought to live' (Laborde, 2017, p. 197). Body-builders, of course, do believe that they ought to shape and preserve their bodies in certain ways, but the 'ought' they thereby follow is just a hypothetical imperative – an 'ought' premised only on a preference they happen to hold. It isn't the categorical kind of 'ought' that Orthodox Jews believe they must follow when they demand an exemption from an autopsy requirement. To say this, however, isn't to imply that one must be religious in order to be bound by imperatives of a categorical nature. Laborde's integrity-based defence of religious exemptions doesn't imply that only religious persons can be entitled to exemptions: atheists with deep ethical or moral commitments also qualify for consideration.[3]

I think the integrity of religious believers is a promising basis for why the law should, under certain circumstances, grant exemptions to religious commitments.[4] But I want to raise some questions about how Laborde spells out the integrity-based argument for exemptions. These questions add up to the following, general point. Laborde's account may be too generous in the way in which it identifies the scope of commitments in which a person's integrity is implicated. In particular, I believe Laborde's account is insufficiently demanding in terms of the other-regarding attitudes it expects people to have before they can make claims to exemptions by appealing to their integrity. This is because on Laborde's account, while the value of integrity does not always trump the interests of others – and so does not support exemptions for religious people who wish to treat others indecently – a person's integrity can, at least, tell in favour of his being exempted from a requirement not to treat others indecently. I believe that this claim should be rejected and that we should endorse a 'moralised' account of integrity, according to which whether the value of a religious person's integrity is threatened at all in an exemption decision is something that depends on whether the practice he wishes to perform complies with certain moral constraints.

Laborde's non-moralised account of integrity

Laborde's account of religious exemptions employs a two-pronged test for determining whether a practice should be exempted from a generally applicable legal regulation. The first stage of the test assesses the value of the practice in question. Laborde puts the question at issue in the first stage as follows: '[w]hat is it about religious claims that justifies the special concern exhibited in exemptions from general law?' To pass this first stage, a given practice must contain 'specific normative values that the law has reason to protect' (Laborde, 2017, p. 195). Once this first stage is passed, we next assess whether the law has adequate reason to refuse exempting the practice in question. I will concentrate on Laborde's explanation of the first stage of test. It is here that she invokes the idea of integrity. She believes that because the law has reason to refrain from undermining the integrity of persons, and because the integrity of religious persons depends on their being able to perform religious practices, the law has a *pro tanto* reason to exempt their religious practices from its otherwise applicable regulations.

For Laborde, a person lives with integrity if, and only if, that person's actions conform to that person's *own* religious convictions. When determining whether a religious claimant's integrity is at stake, courts must therefore follow what she calls a *Thick Sincerity* test (Laborde, 2017, p. 199). They must ask of the given religious practice under consideration whether it is demanded by a religious claimant's religion as that religion is interpreted not by other members of his religious community, but by the claimant himself. When Laborde qualifies the kind of sincerity that is necessary as *thick* sincerity, she means that a religious claimant's convictions must view the practice the claimant wishes to perform as having a certain categorical status. The relevant practice must be *non-trivial* – i.e. 'not simply a whim, preference or unreflected prejudice' and *important* – i.e. it 'not simply a peripheral, incidental or occasional commitment' (Laborde, 2017, p. 200).

Acting in conformity with their own religious convictions, then, is a necessary condition for persons to live with integrity. The question I want to discuss is whether this condition is sufficient as well. On this question, Laborde is not fully clear, but the most reasonable reading of her account is that conformity of action with conviction is, indeed, sufficient.[5] This is made clear, in particular, in Laborde's discussion of why there may not be a religious exemption for infant sacrifice: 'One could suggest', she writes, 'that morally abhorrent claims are flatly incompatible with the pursuit of integrity. People of integrity cannot do abhorrent things...' (Laborde, 2017, p. 201). This line of argument is one that she explicitly *rejects* because she believes that a sincere commitment to performing infant sacrifice can indeed be what she calls an 'integrity-protecting commitment' (Laborde, 2017, p. 202). Laborde obviously does not believe that infant sacrifice should be accommodated, but her reason for denying that it should be accommodated is that it is morally abhorrent, not that the integrity of the practitioner of infant sacrifice is not at stake in his performing it.

Because it does not build moral constraints into the definition of integrity, Laborde's account of integrity is a 'non-moralised' account of integrity. The contrasting account, which holds that the value of integrity depends on the practitioner's complying with certain moral constraints, is a 'moralised' account. Before discussing a problem for the non-moralised account of integrity, it may be helpful to note how the two accounts differ in their practical implications.

Both accounts agree on the thick sincerity test, but they imply that courts should follow different procedures once they have established that the religious claimant meets that test. On the moralised account, courts must ask whether the religious practice in question meets certain moral constraints. If it does not, the religious person's claim lacks the requisite standing, since his integrity is not at stake, and courts can conclude that there is no integrity-based case for exemption. If, by contrast, the practice *does* meet certain moral constraints, the religious person's integrity is at stake, and the moralised account requires courts to proceed to a second stage of reasoning in which they ask whether the interests protected by the law are sufficiently weighty to justify overriding the claimant's integrity. The non-moralised account recommends a different procedure. Once the religious claimant's thick sincerity has been established, courts must proceed straight to the second stage, where they balance interests. The non-moralised account recommends that courts skip over the first stage of the moralised account because it says that we must credit all religious claimants with integrity. Laborde's version of the non-moralised accounts has a twist, insofar as it builds in an exception to this fasttrack procedure: if the practice under consideration is morally abhorrent (e.g. infant sacrifice) we don't fasttrack to the balancing stage, but issue an immediate denial of exemption. Whether there is a difference between the practical implications of the moralised and non-moralised accounts of integrity thus depends on how a proponent of the moralised account defines the 'moral constraints' that a religious practice must meet in order to for the integrity of the claimant to be at stake and how Laborde defines the category of the 'non-abhorrent'. If these two terms are defined in the same way, then there is no practical difference between the accounts. They would allow the same practices to proceed to the second stage of deliberation, where interests are balanced.[6]

A problem for the non-moralised account

I would now like to raise a problem for the non-moralised accounts of integrity. Stated in the most general terms, the problem is that a non-moralised account does not adequately serve the purpose that an account of the basis of a religious exemption must serve. Such an account must show us that the practices that merit religious exemption are, in some way, valuable or worthy of our respect. An account of religious exemptions that appeals to integrity aims to shows us just this: it says that religious practices are valuable or worthy of respect because they enable persons to achieve conformity between their actions and their deepest convictions about how they must live. But I believe that the capacity of an integrity-based account to show us that religious practices are valuable or worthy of respect, and thus justifiably exempted from regulation, is undermined if that account characterises integrity in non-moralised terms.

Consider, again, the example of infant sacrifice. Laborde believes that this practice, even though it is abhorrent, is one that a person's integrity may require him to perform. The trouble is that integrity, in this case, doesn't seem valuable or respect-worthy at all. Our attitude towards another person's conviction that he must perform infant sacrifice is not one of respect that, in the absence of counter-veiling considerations, would prompt us to act with forbearance and accommodation. The conviction that he must sacrifice an infant seems rather to resemble a horrible psychological affliction for him. (If acted upon, it would of course also be a profound evil for the infant who is sacrificed.)[7]

Laborde is aware of this problem. But I am not sure her reply to it succeeds. She writes:

> If individuals are sincerely committed to the pursuit of a wicked cause, they can still be said to act with integrity: it simply means that integrity is one value among others, not the paramount or overriding value...So it is not correct to say, as some have, that because individuals possessing personal integrity may be wicked, integrity is without value. There is value in people pursuing the subjectively-held projects and commitments that are central to their life and worldview – but the pursuit of integrity cannot justify the performance of morally abhorrent actions. (Laborde, 2017, p. 202)

Laborde's reasoning is, I take it, the following. We want to deny, of course, that someone who wishes to perform infant sacrifice should get an exemption; we could deny this, while recognising that this person's integrity requires him to perform infant sacrifice, by denying that integrity matters. But, Laborde notes that we need not deny that integrity matters in order to deny that this person should receive an exemption. We need only assert that there is some superior value that outweighs the value of his integrity (such as the life of the infant). While I agree that the position Laborde endorses here can deliver the desired conclusion regarding whether exemptions should be granted, I do not think it is fully satisfactory. Laborde's position only answers one challenge raised by the example of a person whose religion requires him to perform clearly morally impermissible acts, i.e. that attributing value to integrity must be mistaken because it compels us to exempt evil actions (e.g. infant sacrifice).[8] It does not answer a different challenge that the example of such a person raises for a defence of religious accommodation that appeals to integrity, namely this: attributing value to integrity must be mistaken because there is *nothing* valuable in someone's performing infant sacrifice – not even the sheer fact of his complying with his conviction. That objection remains, and the worry that it generates thus remains as well, namely that integrity is just not valuable as such.

I think that objection is powerful. Although it raises complex issues that I cannot aim to settle here, let me make two brief suggestions in support of it. First, we can test our intuitions by imagining a scenario in which a person manages to conform to his wicked convictions, but without bringing about horrible consequences. Suppose, he sincerely believes he must press a button that causes infant sacrifice by electrocution, but that when he presses the button, the system malfunctions and the infant survives. How should we react to this scenario? It seems odd to think of it as a happy scenario (at least a person has acted in conformity with his convictions!). The more natural reaction is that there is nothing respect-worthy or valuable in what he has done, and that, if anything, he shows signs of a deep psychological affliction that we should try to help him overcome.

The second point is that we can question the examples given in favour of the non-moralised value of integrity. A famous example from Bernard Williams, which Laborde, following Lenta, cites (Laborde, 2017, p. 202), is 'the fanatical Nazi who refused bribes which he was offered to save Jews'.[9] The Nazi, some might say, possesses a valuable kind of integrity, even if the value of his remaining corruption-free (by refusing bribes) is vastly outweighed by the importance of saving Jews. My reaction is that it is only semantically apt to say of the Nazi that he possesses integrity and that there is nothing valuable or respect-worthy to be found in his conduct. In complying with his moral conviction that he must avoid corruption, the Nazi displays an inability to adjust his moral priorities to the overwhelmingly more important cause of saving innocent lives, and this evinces a profound insensitivity to the suffering of innocent people.

Laborde's objections to the moralised account

That the non-moralised account of integrity is not entirely problem-free does not, of course, settle the case in favour of the moralised account. We first need to consider the problems the latter account might face. As I noted earlier, Laborde considers and rejects the moralised account. Let me now examine two objections that Laborde raises against the moralised account of integrity.

(a) *The subjective theory of religious freedom*. Laborde states the first objection briefly as follows: the moralised account of integrity 'is not compatible with a subjective theory of freedom of religion' (Laborde, 2017, p. 202). By a 'subjective theory of freedom of religion', Laborde means a theory 'according to which only individuals – not the state, nor collective religious authorities – are entitled to determine what is the correct interpretation of religious, or more broadly moral, demands on them' (Laborde, 2017, p. 63).

To assess this objection, we should distinguish two different dimensions of a given practice about which a theory of religious freedom might be subjective – i.e. dimensions of that practice with regard to which we should defer to the beliefs of the religious claimant. A subjective theory of freedom of religion may require deference to the religious claimant's beliefs about whether a given practice is, firstly, a religious demand for him, or it may require, secondly, that we defer to a claimant's beliefs about whether the given practice that his religion demands of him is valuable or respect-worthy.

I agree with Laborde that we should endorse the first version of the subjective theory. Courts should not defer to persons other than the religious claimant himself when deciding whether to accept his claim that a given practice is a religious demand for him. (Courts need not, of course, just take a person at his word about this – it may be reasonable for courts to assess his sincerity by asking questions, for example, about the steadfastness of his past commitment to honouring the religious demand in question.). However, the moralised account is compatible with this first version of the subjective theory. According to the moralised account, the value of integrity is limited to the performance of certain kinds of practices, those which are constrained by certain moral criteria. Provided that the practice the religious claimant wishes to perform meets those criteria, the moralised account can recommend that the court proceed straight to the balancing stage, without first asking whether authority figures within the claimant's community accept that the practice is actually required by his religion. So whether or not courts should defer to the claimant or authority figures within his community about that issue isn't something over which the moralised and non-moralised accounts of integrity disagree.

The moralised account of integrity *is* incompatible, however, with the second version of the subjective theory of religious freedom identified above, according to which courts must defer to the religious claimant about whether engaging in a given practice is *valuable or respect-worthy*. By insisting that the practice must meet certain moral criteria before the claimant's integrity can be said to be at stake, the moralised account is, in effect, insisting that it is insufficient that the claimant *himself* regard the practice as valuable or respect-worthy. However, Laborde is not explicit about why its being inconsistent with the second version of the subjective theory of religious freedom would be a problem for the moralised account.[10] But she may implicitly have in mind the following problem of incoherence. The reason we have for insisting that the religious claimant himself, and not authority figures within his community, must be allowed to settle whether a practice is a religious demand for him, also seems to justify that he must be allowed to settle whether that practice is valuable or respect-worthy in a way necessary for his integrity to be at stake. After all, if he should be recognized as a source of religious conviction who is independent from the authority figures within his community, should he not also be recognized as independent from the wider political community – represented by the court – in determining what practices are valuable or respect-worthy? So, once we endorse the first version of the subjective theory – as I agree, with Laborde, we must – we may seem committed to endorsing the second version, too, and hence, on grounds of coherence, to rejecting the moralised account of integrity.

I don't think that's correct. To say, as the moralised account can and should say, that a religious claimant should be allowed to settle what counts as a religious demand for him does not commit a proponent of the moralised account to also saying that the religious claimant must be able to settle whether the practice he wishes to perform meets the moral constraints with which it must comply in order for his integrity to be at stake. That we should recognize each other's independence *within* the sphere permitted by moral constraints does not imply that we should recognize each other's independence in setting the moral constraints themselves. It is not incoherent, therefore, for courts to insist that a religious claimant must be independent from authority figures within his community, while insisting that he may not also settle the moral constraints that practices must meet before the courts must acknowledge that their exercise is a matter for his integrity.

(b) *Reasonable disagreement*. Laborde's second main objection to the moralised account is implicit in how she characterizes the advantage that she believes the non-moralised account of integrity has over the moralised account. One advantage of not moralising integrity, she explains, is that it 'allows us to take seriously reasonable disagreement about liberal justice' (Laborde, 2017, p. 203). It does this because it allows courts to consider awarding exemptions to claims, which, while not morally abhorrent, are nevertheless, 'morally ambivalent'. These are claims 'that can be fitted into one or other recognizably liberal conception of justice', for example a claim to 'inflict mild corporal punishment on one's children' (Laborde, 2017, p. 203). Because Laborde's non-moralised account of integrity allows that religious claimants can live with integrity when performing practices that not all recognize as morally acceptable, it takes seriously the fact that citizens can reasonable disagree about justice and the good life.

The implicit objection against the moralised account, I take it, is that it fails to do this. Because it holds that claims to exemption turn on whether the practices in question meet certain moral constraints, the moralised account implies that courts should enter into a moral evaluation of, say, mild corporal punishment for children and, if they conclude that the practice fails certain moral constraints, deny that parents who wish to perform this practice have integrity at stake. But this does not take seriously the fact that people can reasonably disagree about the moral acceptability of mild corporate punishment for children.

I do not think that the concern that courts – and the political community, more generally – should take seriously reasonable disagreement is relevant for whether courts must adopt a moralised or non-moralised account of integrity. Consider how courts would have to proceed if they adopted a non-moralised account. After allowing that the integrity of parents who believe they must inflict mild corporate punishment on religious grounds is at stake over whether they can perform that practice, they would have to assess whether the interests protected by the law justify denying the exemption in question. It is hard to see how, in doing this, a court would be doing anything substantively different from what the moralised account says it must do. Suppose a court concludes that the child's interests in avoiding pain and psychological trauma are too great to justify allowing parents to inflict mild corporal punishment, even if the parents hold deep convictions that they must. It would seem untruthful of a court to communicate the verdict as follows: 'We think the trauma to your children is too great to justify your doing this even if your integrity is at stake, but we are not saying that your doing it would be morally unacceptable'. Surely that *is* what the court is saying. The non-moralised account thus seems to allow the court to override the parents' view about the moral status of mild corporal punishment on the basis of its own moral verdict about that matter. It only does this at a different stage of deliberation from when it would do it if it proceeded on the basis of the moralized account. So it is difficult to see the sense in which courts, by following the non-moralised account, would take reasonable disagreement any more seriously than they would were they to follow the moralised account.

Integrity as responsiveness

I would now like to say something more foundational in support of the moralised account. My point of departure is the suggestion that it seems mistaken to think that the value we are trying to capture with the term 'integrity' should turn *only* on a fit between actions and deep conviction. Consider the following bizarre example:

> *Hypnotized homophobia.* Henry has been hypnotized into holding a deep conviction that his God requires him to act in ways that express condemnation of homosexuality. Acting on this belief, he refuses to let out his property to a homosexual couple.

The question is whether Henry's integrity is at stake over the issue of whether he should be exempted from a generally applicable prohibition against discrimination on grounds of sexual orientation. Now, if *all* that mattered for his integrity were that he acts in line with his deep religious conviction, we would have to answer, 'yes'. But this seems like the wrong answer. Whatever it is whose value we are trying to capture with the term, 'integrity', it doesn't seem present in Henry's case.[11]

What's missing? As well as consisting of enactment – i.e. of pressing conviction into action, integrity consists of responsiveness – of one's trying to figure out how one must live according to some standard or standards of ultimate value that one regards as having authority over oneself. To say something more specific about what such responsiveness might consist in, it is helpful to consider what it is we tend to regard as valuable or respect-worthy in straightforward cases of persons who act with integrity, for example a case in which officials resist strong pressure to disregard the interests of vulnerable people. What we admire about these officials, and what we name with the word 'integrity', is the fact that they are not allowing themselves to be swayed by considerations by which they ought not to be swayed. Integrity seems to consist, in other words, of a certain kind of resoluteness, a strong disposition to insulate oneself from considerations by which one should not, ideally, be affected, or, put more positively, to render oneself sensitive to the considerations that genuinely matter (or, in other words, that matter from an objective point of view). Drawing on this idea, we could say that integrity consists of forming and sustaining one's convictions in a way that is consistent with the most basic demands of justice, such as, for example, the demand that we respect the dignity of all persons.[12]

Why exactly would construing integrity in this way imply a moralised account of integrity – i.e. an account that sets moral constraints to the kinds of practices that should be considered as implicating a religious claimant's integrity? If the value of integrity consist in our good faith efforts at being responsive to the most basic demands of justice, then a relevant question about any given practice under consideration is whether the claimant's conviction that he must perform it is one that he could have formed, and could plausibly be sustaining, out of a good faith effort to comply with the most basic demands of justice. For example, there is overwhelming reason to suspect that a person who wishes to perform infant sacrifice has failed to form that conviction in a manner that is sensitive to the dignity of the infant he wishes to sacrifice. We should therefore conclude that there is no integrity at stake, here, because this person has not tried to constrain himself by the most basic demands of justice.

Infant sacrifice, of course, is an easy example with which to illustrate the plausibility of an account. So let's take a more controversial example that involves a religious person who is hostile to homosexuals but who, unlike Henry, has not been hypnotised into that hostility. In my view, we may have good enough reason to suspect of some religious people who manifest hostile attitudes towards homosexuals that they do not sustain those attitudes from a good faith effort at being responsive to the most basic demands of justice. For example, a court might establish that a particular religious claimant merely wishes to manifest homophobic prejudice (as opposed to a belief formed in good faith, that he must dissociate from homosexuals), say, by obtaining evidence that this claimant has regularly displayed hostile behaviour towards homosexuals in other contexts, where such hostile behaviour is not actually warranted by his religious beliefs (even as he himself would explain those beliefs). This evidence might lead the court to the conclusion that his anti-homosexual religious beliefs cannot be plausibly seen as a result of his taking seriously, among other considerations, the fundamental idea, which the court regards as objectively true, that all human beings have dignity. This doesn't mean that courts should disqualify *all* anti-homosexual religious beliefs as incompatible with integrity. Some religious claimants with anti-homosexual beliefs may well be able to demonstrate that they have taken seriously the idea that all human beings have dignity and their integrity may well be at stake, then, in whether or not they can disassociate from homosexuals. The point I am making is that we should not automatically assume that all anti-homosexual religious beliefs are compatible with the integrity of the religious believer.

One challenge for this way of thinking about the value of integrity is that we disagree about the objective moral constraints that courts should expect religious claimants to take seriously. That is certainly true, but the moral constraints that courts should insist upon need not be constraints over which people can reasonably disagree, but could be restricted to those over which people cannot reasonably disagree, such as the idea that all human beings have dignity.

A deeper challenge, which, for lack of space I can only register here, is this: one may think that it is sufficient for integrity that a person form and sustain his convictions in response to considerations that *he thinks* matter rather than considerations that objectively matter. My inclination is to deny this, and to assert that integrity is a kind of success that we achieve one when we strive, in good faith, to respond to the considerations that objectively matter in how we live our lives. A person who believes he must sacrifice an infant is someone who fails in this regard, either because he is not sustaining his beliefs in good faith, of, if he is, because he lacks a basic competence to appreciate the worth of the infant. And it is also my inclination to say that less extreme forms of indecency, such as some forms of homophobic religiosity, can also be failures in this regard. But much more needs to be said, of course, in support of this inclination, if we are to fully spell out the basis for the moralised account of integrity.

Let me conclude with a suggestion about why the difference between the moralised and non-moralised account of integrity matters. As I noted earlier, it is possible that the two accounts differ very little from each other, if at all, in their practical implications. Still, the moralised account tells us something that the non-moralised does not, namely, that we should not recognize it as *in any way* valuable – and neither should our political institutions, including our courts – that some members of our political community wish to comply with convictions that fail to show a certain basic consideration for others. That difference is important because we owe it to those to whom gross moral insensitivity is shown not to sanctify that insensitivity. But it is important also for another reason. Refusing to recognise as valuable a person's compliance with his own gross moral insensitivity is something that we owe also to that person himself, at least if he is able to do better. It expresses to him that we expect him to be, and regard him as capable of being, a full member of our moral community.

Notes

1. The example is discussed by Laborde (2017, p. 213). As Laborde points out, the original source of the example is Galston and Greenawalt (2008, p. 315).
2. The body-builder example is my illustration of Laborde's view, not one that she provides herself.
3. I use the term 'ethical' to refer to matters pertaining to the good life, and 'moral' to matters pertaining to what we owe to each other.
4. For other writers who have endorsed an integrity-based justification of religious exemption, see Bou-Habib (2006), Maclure and Taylor (2011), and Lenta (2016).
5. Laborde implies, at one point, that an additional condition is necessary for integrity, which she calls *Thin Acceptability*, and by which she means that a practice must meet certain very basic criteria of moral decency. She asks, 'which test should judges use to assess integrity? I set out two tests, which I call *Thick Sincerity* and *Thin Acceptability*' (Laborde, 2017, p. 199). But, as I now explain, if we attend to what Laborde explicitly says elsewhere, it is clear that she does not, in fact, regard Thin Acceptability as a test of integrity.
6. Although the moralised and non-moralised accounts support the same judgements in these cases, and so appealing to these cases does not settle the case in favour of the moralised account, my arguments in what follows aim to do just that.
7. For another source of skepticism of the view that compliance with deep conviction is valuable or respect-worthy as such, see Koppelman (2009).
8. This is the version of the objection that Koppelman raises. See (Koppelman, 2009, p. 222).
9. The quote is from Lenta (2016, p. 254).
10. Laborde may not think that *this* is a problem for the moralised account. She may think the problem with the account is only that it is inconsistent with the first version of the subjective theory of religious freedom. But, as I just pointed out, I don't think it is.

11. I am here adapting a version of an objection to the so-called 'hierarchical' account of autonomy raised by Mele (2001, pp. 147–8). According to the hierarchical account, it is sufficient for autonomous action that the agent's first-order desire to perform that action is endorsed, in some way, by a second-order volition. See Frankfurt (1988, pp. 12–25). As Mele points out, however, how the second-order volition itself came about also seems relevant for autonomous action. See also Christman (1991).
12. I am grateful to an anonymous referee for helping me to formulate this view more precisely.

Disclosure statement

No potential conflict of interest was reported by the author.

References

Bou-Habib, P. (2006). A theory of religious accommodation. *Journal of Applied Philosophy, 23*(1), 109–126.

Christman, J. (1991). Autonomy and personal history. *Canadian Journal of Philosophy, 21*(1), 1–24.

Frankfurt, H. (1988). *The importance of what we care about*. Cambridge: Cambridge University Press.

Galston, W., & Greenawalt, K. (2008). *Religion and the constitution*. Princeton: Princeton University Press.

Koppelman, A. (2009). Conscience, volitional necessity, and religious exemptions. *Legal Theory, 15*(2), 215–244.

Laborde, C. (2017). *Liberalism's religion*. Cambridge, MA: Harvard University Press.

Lenta, P. (2016). Freedom of conscience and the value of personal integrity. *Ratio Juris, 29*(2), 246–263.

Maclure, J., & Taylor, C. (2011). *Secularism and freedom of conscience*. Cambridge, MA: Harvard University Press.

Mele, A. (2001). *Autonomous agents: From self-control to autonomy*. New York and Oxford: Oxford University Press.

Individual integrity, freedom of association and religious exemption

Peter Jones

> **ABSTRACT**
> Of the many questions Cécile Laborde addresses in her magisterial *Liberalism's Religion*, several relate to what she describes as 'the puzzle of exemptions'. I examine some of the issues raised by her efforts to solve that puzzle: whether her ideal of moral integrity squares with the nature of religious belief; whether we should find the case for collective religious exemptions in freedom of association and the 'coherence interests' of associations; how much significance we should give to the 'competence interests' of organised religions; and by which criteria we should assess individual claims to religious exemption.

Introduction

Liberalism's relationship to religion has long been a matter of debate not only between liberals and their critics but also amongst liberals themselves. In Cécile Laborde's *Liberalism's Religion*, we have a major contribution to that debate distinguished by its comprehensive treatment of the subject, the sheer range of scholarship with which it engages, and the rigour and originality of its reasoning. It is the kind of book that reviewers will insist no future student of the subject can ignore – and this time they will be right. I could happily devote the following pages to cataloguing of all there is to admire and applaud in *Liberalism's Religion*, but that would be tedious for the reader and not what is expected for a symposium of this sort. In political philosophy, the time-honoured way in which we celebrate someone's intellectual achievement is by trying to find fault with it and in some measure I shall follow that tradition. However the piecemeal nature of my criticism indicates the difficulty I have had in finding quarrels to pick with Laborde, and much of what I say is observation on, rather than dissent from, the positions for which she argues. My comments focus on what Laborde describes as 'the puzzle of exemptions', a puzzle that arises repeatedly throughout the pages of *Liberalism's Religion* but one with which she grapples most directly in Chapters 5 and 6.

Integrity and religious exemption

Laborde argues that religious practices are *pro tanto* candidates for exemption not because they are specifically religious but because and insofar as they are ethically salient. Ethically salient non-religious practices are therefore also *pro tanto* candidates for exemption. The emphasis Laborde places on ethical salience as the relevant feature of religious practices that makes them eligible for exemption is, I believe, entirely justified. However, she is not content to rest her case there. She moves on to an idea of moral integrity as the justifying foundation of religious exemption and it is the need for and the appropriateness of that move that I want to begin by questioning.

She describes the commitments for which exemptions provide as 'integrity-protecting commitments'. 'Commitments' refer to practices or conduct in which the committed person believes she ought to engage. 'An integrity-protecting commitment is a commitment, manifested in a practice, ritual, or action (or refusal to act) that allows an individual to live in accordance with how she thinks she ought to live' (pp. 203–204).[1] The description 'integrity-protecting' indicates that individuals' ability or freedom to adhere to their commitments both *protects* their integrity and *matters* because it protects their integrity. What then is integrity? Laborde describes it as 'an ideal of congruence between one's ethical commitments and one's actions' and cites approvingly Cheshire Calhoun's characterisation of integrity as 'fidelity to those projects and principles that are constitutive of one's identity' (p. 203). Integrity therefore consists in a form of integration; it describes a condition of coherence between one's ethical beliefs or convictions and one's actions. If I cannot do what I believe I should, I suffer a loss of integrity; my life will not exhibit the coherence that ideally it would. Integrity is 'primarily a formal relation one has to oneself, or between parts or aspects of one's self' (p. 203). This idea of an integrated self, or an integrated life, might easily be applied to the congruence a person might enjoy between her needs or preferences and her ability to satisfy them, but Laborde limits the scope of integrity to 'ethical commitments'. Her notion of integrity therefore combines the two ordinary-language senses of the term: acting ethically and exhibiting a condition of harmony or coherence.

In placing integrity at the centre of her account, Laborde intentionally emphasises the subjective orientation of her account and its focus on the selfhood of the believer. Integrity underwrites a 'subjective theory of freedom of religion' (p. 204). It requires people to 'act out of their own convictions', that is, out of convictions with which they 'deeply identify' (p. 204);

'the content of integrity ... cannot be drawn from any objective, person-independent conception of the good: it can only be defined by the individual whose integrity is at stake.' (pp. 204). In satisfying a court of their sincerity, those who claim an exemption must show that the practice at issue 'touches on something that is connected to their sense of self, to their moral or ethical identity' (p. 207). 'Ultimately', for Laborde, 'the value of integrity is grounded in values of identity, autonomy, moral agency and self-respect' (p. 204). She denies that her integrity-based defence of exemptions is 'sectarian'; rather it can be embraced by both the religious and the non-religious alike. With Paul Bou-Habib (2006), she believes that the value of integrity enables non-religious people to understand what is so special for religious people about being able to practise their religion, and she endorses his view that the integrity-defence enables the religious to instantiate in their life 'something they themselves value as moral agents: their integrity' (p. 204, quoting Bou-Habib).

Given that Laborde is seeking to provide for exemptions in a context of religious and non-religious pluralism and to do so in a liberal egalitarian fashion, her 'subjective' approach to the case for exemptions is unsurprising. However, I want to suggest that it is unnecessarily and inappropriately subjective for the task at hand. To keep the issue manageable, I consider only religious claims to exemption. In doing so, I do not mean to dissent from Laborde's argument that religious claims to exemption are most plausible and compelling when they take the form of ethical claims. I agree that it is as ethical claims in general, rather only religious claims in particular, that they have a character and status that distinguishes them from mere preferences or non-ethical conceptions of the good. As Laborde observes, people cannot sacrifice their ethical commitments 'without feelings of remorse, shame or guilt, by contrast to preferences, which can' (p. 204) – which is not to suggest that the bad of acting wrongly consists in experiencing those feelings, but to indicate that being subject to a moral requirement is different from merely having a preference. But, if we have managed to establish that ethical claims can ground a *pro tanto* case for exemption in a way that non-ethical claims cannot and that religious claims, insofar as they are ethical, share in that case, do we need to take a further step and embrace Laborde's ideal of integrity? I want to suggest that we do not and that, if we do, we can misrepresent the way in which people stand to their religious beliefs and commitments.

People's religious beliefs are typically objective in conception in that they are beliefs about what is true of the world and how we should conduct our lives. In particular, the norms that should govern our conduct are not exercises in self-legislation but divinely sanctioned norms that have been laid down for us. Of course, for any particular religious adherent, the religion that provides the 'objective, person-independent conception of the good' that properly governs his conduct will be the religion to which he subscribes, but, for the religious adherent, what makes his religion the religion that properly governs his conduct is not the fact that he subscribes to it.

That may be true of how people conceive their relation to what it is they believe in, but it may still be the case that what is of value, what matters about, their acting in accordance with the norms of their religion is the securing or maintenance of their integrity. However, that would be an oddly 'self-centred' reason for complying with what the religious adherent conceives as an objectively-given, moral imperative. The much more obvious reason she has for compliance is simply that that it is what she should do. Her reason for complying with the imperative is not *her believing* that it is the right thing to do and her wish that her actions should comport with her beliefs, but simply that it *is* (she believes) the right thing to do. If she asks for an exemption that will enable to her to engage in a practice which (she believes) God requires, her reason for doing so is most obviously her wanting to do what (she believes) God requires. It is not her wanting to maintain her integrity, even though the effect of the exemption, if granted, may be to secure her integrity.

Laborde often associates integrity with identity. I act with integrity when I am true to myself, when I am faithful to who I really am. Doubtless people's beliefs, especially their religious beliefs, can contribute significantly to their sense of identity and to the identity that others project onto them. But it would be odd to think of an identity as a reason for holding, or for acting on, a belief, especially if it is a religious belief. As I have argued elsewhere (Jones, 1999, pp. 81–83), it would be an odd Muslim who, having protested that Mohammed was God's Prophet and that the Koran was the Word of God, or an odd Christian who, having affirmed that Jesus Christ was God incarnate and that salvation lay in faith in Him, then went on to insist that what really mattered about those beliefs was their contribution to his identity. It may be that, in a religiously plural society, the very plurality of beliefs induces people to conceive their own beliefs in more subjective terms and to reach for the language of integrity and identity in demanding respect from others. But giving primacy to integrity and identity remains an odd move for those who take their religious beliefs seriously both as *religious* beliefs and as religious *beliefs*.

Religious associations and collective exemptions

Laborde also appeals to integrity in making the case for collective religious exemptions and in establishing what those exemptions should be. However, her argument in the collective case is caught up with her claim that 'whatever exemption rights religious associations should have are derived from the liberal value of freedom of association' (p. 161; similarly p. 171). The exemptions with which she is primarily concerned are exemptions from laws that prohibit discrimination in employment and in the provision of goods and services on grounds such as race, gender and sexual orientation.

In making the case for collective religious exemptions, Laborde distinguishes two sorts of interest that can give an association a claim to exemption: coherence and competence interests. The *coherence* interests of associations consist in their 'ability to *live by* their own standards, purposes and commitments'; their *competence* interests lie in their 'ability to *interpret* their own standards, purposes and commitments' (p. 175, my emphases). These interests justify exemptions of different sorts (pp. 175–176). A religious association's coherence interests can justify its being exempt from laws that are otherwise general in application, such as an exemption granted to the Catholic Church from laws prohibiting gender discrimination so that it can appoint only men to its priesthood. A religious association's competence interest can justify special treatment of a rather different kind. It can require courts to defer to an association's judgement on what its doctrines, commitments or standards require, because the association has a competence on those matters that a court does not. While these two interests may justify exemptions for religious associations, neither justification is unique to religious associations. I comment first on Laborde's idea of coherence interests. My principal doubt about this part of her argument concerns her claim that the case for collective religious exemptions derives from the value of freedom of association. Contrary to her view, I suggest that the justification for collective religious exemption owes more to freedom of religion than to freedom of association.

Coherence interests and exemption

The coherence interests of an association lie in its ability to live by its own standards, purposes and commitments. An association exists to pursue a conception of the good and individuals join it to share in that pursuit. Associations provide structures that make that shared pursuit possible. Their coherence interests are their interests in sustaining their integrity, where 'integrity' means 'their ability to maintain a structure through which their members can pursue the purpose for which they have associated' (p. 178).

On my understanding of Laborde's analysis, the set of associations that possess coherence interests is larger than the set that are candidates for exemption. Indeed, given that all formally structured associations (the form of 'association' at issue here) have purposes, implicit if not explicit, perhaps all have coherence interests.[2] What then distinguishes the associations that are eligible for exemptions? Laborde identifies two features. First, they must be voluntary associations. In particular, an association's members must be free to leave the association without undue cost; only then can we be sure that people's continued membership is voluntary. Secondly, the association must be 'identificatory'. It must be the kind of group 'that individuals join to pursue a conception of the good that is central to their identity and integrity' (p.174).

These two features relate to the justification of exemptions in different ways. The first is more akin to a qualifying condition. Its rationale according to Laborde is that exemptions give associations power over their members; if an exemption enables an association to discriminate on grounds such as gender or sexual orientation, the voluntariness of its membership is an essential to safeguard for those who find themselves subject to that discrimination (p. 181). The second feature, the identificatory nature of the association, has a more justificatory character. An association is identificatory if its individual members 'identify with the projects and commitments that are at the core of the association's integrity'; it allows its members 'to integrate core aspects of their personal beliefs and commitments with associational goals and values' (p. 182).

I have misgivings about the adjective 'identificatory'; it seems too imprecise, contingent and potentially inclusive a term to mark off associations that are credible candidates for exemption. If, however, we overlook that issue and focus on Laborde's reference to the way in which the goals and values of the association relate to core aspects of its members' personal beliefs and commitments, that would seem to imply that it is the nature of the association's standards, commitments and purposes that distinguishes it as an association that is eligible for exemptions. Just as the ethical nature of individuals' religious commitments makes them candidates for individual exemptions, so the ethical nature of the standards, purposes and commitments of religious associations makes them candidates for collective exemptions. Indeed, it would be puzzling if a commitment's eligibility for exemption turned fundamentally on whether it took an individual or collective form. Of course, the specific content of exemptions may differ, simply because there are many things that people can do collectively that they cannot do individually, such as stage collective acts of worship or create structures of authority, but that is no reason why their basic justification should differ. The most obvious justification for collective religious exemptions is the same as that for individual religious exemptions, in which case it is freedom of religion rather than freedom of association that justifies collective religious exemptions.

Laborde seems unwilling to settle for that simple view. In line with her idea of coherence interests and the integrity of associations, she argues that identificatory associations are distinguished by their 'mode' of association. They exhibit an unusually 'tight' coherence between their purpose, structure, membership and public. Persons involved in the working of the association, whether they are leaders, members, employees or customers, are in 'the right (identificatory) relationship with the association'. (p. 184). That gives the association a key interest in its coherence and one that, for Laborde, justifies its claim to exemption. In fairness to Laborde, I should note that much of what she says in this part of her argument is geared to issues raised by the US *Hobby Lobby* case and the need to distinguish between associations whose combined religious and commercial purposes do, and those whose combined purposes do not, jeopardise their eligibility for exemption. Her efforts seem designed to uncover an equivalence between the integrity of an association and the integrity of an individual. Her emphasis upon the coherence interests of associations suggests an analogy with her model of the integrated person, whereas the more compelling analogy would be with the model of the ethical person.

Consistently with her view that the exemption rights of religious associations derive from the value of freedom of association and that it is the coherence interests of religious associations that earn them a right to exemption, Laborde seems disinclined to accept that the granting of statutory exemptions to religious associations amounts to a form of 'special treatment'. Thus she writes, 'the Catholic Church's prerogative to exclude women from its clergy is a coherence interest, no different from the prerogative of other associations to enforce and live by their professed standards and principles' (p. 175). Is that really so? Consider the exemption the Equality Act (2010) grants to organised religions allowing them to discriminate in employment on grounds of gender, sexual orientation, gender re-assignment and marital status (Schedule 9, Pt 1, para. 2). The Act allows that discrimination only insofar as it is needed to 'to comply with the doctrines of the religion' (the compliance principle) or to avoid conflict with 'the strongly held religious convictions of a significant number of the religion's followers' (the non-conflict principle).

Laborde's view would seem to be that, for the Catholic Church, discriminating on grounds of gender or sexual orientation in the appointment of clergy is no different in principle from discriminating on grounds religious faith. All of these are relevant occupational qualifications. That is certainly true from the perspective of the Catholic Church but is it, or should it be, true for public policy on discrimination? That policy need have no difficulty in recognising adherence to a church's faith as a proper requirement for appointees to the church's clergy. Under the Equality Act, that adherence would qualify readily as an 'occupational requirement' and one that constituted 'a proportionate means of achieving a legitimate aim' (Schedule 9, Pt 1, s.1). But being of particular gender and sexual orientation are not 'occupational requirements' in the same straightforward sense. In the case of the Catholic Church, they are qualifications for appointment only insofar as they are made so by the doctrines of the Church. Moreover, they are qualifications that run counter to general principles of public policy on discrimination. For public policy, allowing an organised religion to discriminate on grounds of gender or sexual orientation in appointing its clergy constitutes an exemption, while allowing it to require that its clergy should adhere to its religion is not. That is not to say that public policy should not grant the exemption. It is to say only that more is needed to justify it than merely insisting on the freedom of an association (any association) to live by its own standards and principles (Jones, 2015, pp. 553–556).

Competence interests and exemption

While an association's coherence interests relate to its ability to live by its own standards, purposes and commitments, its competence interests concern its special expertise 'in the interpretation and application of those standards, purposes and commitments' (p. 191). One reason for distinguishing these interests is simply that they are different. But another, Laborde argues, is that the set of associations whose competence interests justify special treatment by the courts is smaller than the set whose coherence interests give them a *pro tanto* claim to statutory exemption. Religious associations fall within that smaller set. The inaccessibility of their doctrines to public reason justifies limiting the extent to which courts should interfere in their internal lives (p. 191). Laborde's claim is not that religious associations should be entirely immune from judicial attention; rather it is that a court should afford them a greater 'margin of appreciation' in the interpretation and application of their own standards, purposes and commitments than it would to the general run of associations. Exemption-justifying competence interests, like exemption-justifying coherence interests, are not unique to religious associations. Laborde suggests, for instance, that courts have the same reason to defer to the expertise of universities on issues concerning the scholarly standards appropriate to the selection and promotion of academic staff (pp. 175–176, 194–195).

The case to which Laborde applies her argument most convincingly is that of the selection and dismissal of clergy, insofar as those decisions turn on theologically based judgements of the doctrinal conformity and standards of conduct that a religion properly requires of its clergy (pp. 192–193). If, however, we set the issue of competence in the more general context of British discrimination law, what is equally remarkable is the lack of discretion that law gives organised religions to determine how the exemptions they are granted are to be interpreted and applied. Moreover, that is a state of affairs that Laborde herself would seem largely to endorse.

If once again we take the Catholic Church as our example, the issue here is not whether the state should judge the propriety of the Church's doctrines as religious doctrines or assess whether the Church's current doctrines are authentic expressions of Roman Catholicism. Nor is it whether the Church should be exempt from discrimination law so that it can comply with its own doctrines. We assume that general exemption to be justified and already in place. Against that background, the most obvious issue to which competence interests apply is the proper scope the exemption should have. Over what range of posts should a church be able to require that adherence to its faith is a condition of employment? The application of that requirement to its clergy is unlikely to be controversial. But is its application to a choir-master justified and, if it is, should it also be applicable to the church's administrative staff or to those whom it employs to clean and maintain its buildings? The same questions arise in respect of the exemption of organised religions from laws prohibiting discrimination on grounds such as gender and sexual orientation.

The noteworthy feature of British discrimination law on that question is how closely it regulates the answer. As we noted in the previous section, the Equality Act 2010 permits discrimination only insofar as it is justified by the compliance principle or the non-conflict principle. The Act's explanatory notes add that the exemptions are 'intended to cover a very narrow range of employment: ministers of religion and a small number of lay posts, including those that exist to promote and represent religion' (para. 799). The discriminatory requirement must also be 'crucial to the post and not merely one of several important factors' (para. 800).[3] It falls to the courts to interpret and apply these provisions and, in doing so, they have shown little propensity to defer to the judgements of organised religions.[4]

The narrow scope that British discrimination law gives religious exemptions is largely an artefact of legislation rather than the practice of the judiciary. Laborde invokes competence interests as claims to deference from courts rather than legislatures but that would seem to be an entirely contingent matter. If an association's competence interests generate claims to exemption, there is no obvious reason why those claims should not relate to legislation as well as to judicial practice.

Laborde herself takes US rather than UK law as her principal point of reference but the position she defends differs little from that of current British discrimination law. For very sound reasons she rejects the US doctrine of 'ministerial exception', according to which religious associations should be entirely immune from legal scrutiny in the employment of their ministers (pp. 176–177). She also rejects the claim that religious associations should be able to discriminate on religious grounds across the entire range of their employees. Like the Equality Act (2010), she stresses the distinction between 'core' and 'peripheral' religious activities in identifying when discrimination on grounds of religious faith is and is not justified. Such discrimination should be confined to posts which are devoted to direct engagement in religious work (pp. 185–187).

The claims of competence interests in relation discrimination law would therefore seem very limited. Courts cannot avoid 'entanglement' with religion in administering discrimination law, but that entanglement need not be of an invidious or troubling kind. In the case of British law, courts have to judge whether an organised religion's discrimination is justified by the compliance or non-conflict principle, but those are judgements of fact rather than of 'correct' doctrine or conviction. Courts have also to judge over what range of an organised religion's posts and activities its exemption properly extends, but that too requires a combined factual and legal judgement. It would be a dereliction of duty for a court to hand over those judgements to an organised religion, but there is no reason why it should. The judgements will not always be easy, but that is because the doctrines of an organised religion may be shifting or internally disputed, or because the criterion relating to the convictions of a religion's followers is vaguely formulated, or because the boundary between religious and non-religious activities will sometimes be fuzzy. It will not be because the judgements require abstruse insights into theology to which clerics are privy and courts are not.

Justifying religious exemptions

While Laborde emphasises the importance of integrity to the case for religious exemptions, either individual or collective, she claims only that it delivers a *pro tanto* case. How then are we to decide whether justice demands an exemption all things considered? In answering that question, Laborde distinguishes two different grounds for exemption: disproportionate burden and majority bias.

Disproportionate burden

A society should exempt religious adherents from a law if the law burdens the practice of their religion disproportionately (pp. 221–229). Laborde identifies four types of consideration that we must weigh in determining whether a legal burden is indeed disproportionate. On one side of the balance we have the weight of the burden that the law imposes upon the religious claimant. That weight includes both (i) the 'directness' of the burden – whether the religious practice remains possible at all and, if it does, at what cost to the claimant, and (ii) its 'severity' – how significantly the practice figures in the claimant's religion and therefore how severely its burdening compromises her religion. On the other side is (iii) the importance of the law's aim and how significantly an exemption would frustrate it, and (iv) the costs that an exemption might shift from the claimant onto others. The justice of granting or withholding an exemption turns on how these considerations weigh against one another. We are more accustomed to thinking of justice as a matter of principle than as the outcome of a trade-off, but it is hard to find an acceptable alternative to the weighing process Laborde describes. Courts, in assessing the scope of religious liberty to which people have a human right under the European Convention, engage in just that sort of balancing exercise.

Rather than pursue the issue of balancing any further, I want to comment briefly on how religion can figure differently in the case for an exemption and how that difference might affect our thinking on the all-things-considered case for an exemption. Laborde is primarily concerned with exemptions as instruments that protect and promote religious liberty. So conceived, the goal of an exemption is to secure people's freedom to practise their religion. That is the form that religious exemption takes when it arises out of human rights law in Europe and out of the constitutional right to 'free exercise' in the US.

Religion may, however, figure in an exemption in a different way. The goal which an exemption seeks to secure may be a non-religious good and the burden that the exemption seeks to remove may arise from the conflict between a law or rule and a religious commitment. That is the form that exemption takes when it arises out of law on indirect religious discrimination. The aim of that law is not to secure people's religious liberty but to secure fair opportunities in employment and in access to goods and services. For instance, when an employer's rule conflicts with a person's religious commitment such that it effectively denies an employment opportunity to the person, indirect religious discrimination law requires the employer (subject to certain qualifications) to exempt the religious adherent from the rule. So here the religious practice figures not in the goal of the exemption but as something that combines with an externally imposed rule to burden the attainment of a non-religious good, a burden which discrimination law removes by exempting the religious adherent from the employer's rule.

Consider now an exemption to which Laborde is evidently unsympathetic (p. 218): the exemption of turban-wearing Sikhs from the legal obligation to wear a safety helmet if they ride a motorcycle. Laborde has good reason to be unsympathetic. If we conceive protecting the religious liberty of Sikhs as the goal of the exemption, the case for it is weak. The 'severity' of the burden is significant since it consists in Sikhs having to remove their turbans, but its 'directness' is much less so, since Sikhs can easily comply with their religion by using forms of transport other than motorcycles. The legal obligation of motorcyclists to wear safety helmets cannot therefore be said seriously to impede the practice of the Sikh faith.

But now let's recast that exemption so that its goal becomes enabling Sikhs to ride motorcycles, while the burden that impedes the goal's realisation is the legal requirement that motorcycling Sikhs must, like other motorcyclists, wear safety helmets. Now the burden scores highly on 'directness'; without an exemption, devout Sikhs can attain the goal only by contravening a major commitment of their faith. It is less easy to know how we should characterise the 'severity' of the burden since the burdened activity (motorcycling) is not now a religious practice. I shall not here offer an all-things-considered justification for the exemption. I limit myself to the point that the case for the exemption is different, and I think stronger, if its purpose is to enable Sikhs to ride motorcycles rather than to practise their religion. Another exemption relating to devout Sikhs, to which Laborde is more sympathetic (p. 222), is that enabling them to work on construction sites without wearing safety helmets. But in that instance too the case for the exemption seems more compelling if its goal is conceived – on analogy with indirect religious discrimination law – as protecting an employment opportunity for Sikhs rather than protecting the practice of the Sikh faith.

If we conceive the primary aim of an exemption as other than protection of a religious practice, perhaps we should no longer describe the exemption as 'religious'. But, however we describe it, academic debate on exemptions which remove legal-cum-religious obstacles to the enjoyment of non-religious goods has focused primarily on how we should apportion responsibility for the existence of those obstacles and how their religious nature affects a society's obligation to respond to them.[5]

Majority bias

The justice relevant to disproportionate burden is non-comparative: we do not need to know how a society treats other citizens to know that it treats unjustly a citizen whom it burdens disproportionately. Laborde's test of 'majority bias' (pp. 229–238), by contrast, appeals to an idea of justice that is both comparative and distributive. A society treats a minority unequally and unfairly if it accords the minority fewer core opportunities because its arrangements are biased in favour of the majority's religion. Appeals to equality are conspicuous amongst defenders of exemptions and, arguably, too conspicuous (Jones, 2017). Commentators often take too little account of the *sui generis* character of religious practices and too readily suppose that conflict between a religious practice and a society's public arrangements must evince unequal treatment. That said, distributive considerations obviously matter; it matters not only that people enjoy goods, or do not endure bads, but also that they do so fairly relative to one another. Yet, even when the practices of different religions are sufficiently similar to make comparison possible, it is not always easy to know what fairness demands.

Consider one of the distributive issues Laborde instances (pp. 231–232): a society's conventional non-working day and its coincidence or non-coincidence with the day of the week that is special for a particular religion, such as Sunday for Christians, Saturday for Jews or Friday for Muslims. Does the *reason* why one religion's special day coincides with a society's non-working day make a difference to the claim of those who do not enjoy the same coincidence? Suppose that a society's official non-working day is Tuesday, which is not a day special to any religious group in the society. Then, at a later point in the society's history, a new religious group springs up, or migrates from another society, whose 'sabbath' is Tuesday. Let's call them the Tuesdayers. Is the society then obliged, as a matter of fairness, to accommodate the sabbaths of all of its other religious groups so that those groups are in no way disadvantaged relative to the Tuesdayers? Arguably not, because the Tuesdayers are accidental rather than intended beneficiaries of the society's non-working day and an arrangement that is not intentionally designed to benefit a particular group is misdescribed as 'biased'. The society's non-working day has not been culturally 'formatted' (p. 230) to suit the Tuesdayers. Indeed, we need not resort to fictional examples to illustrate that point. Saturday is a non-working day for many employees in western societies and that (as far as I know) has nothing to do with its being the sabbath of Jews and Seventh Day Adventists. Does, then, the good fortune of Jews and Seventh Day Adventists relative to Muslims require a society to secure legally guaranteed time off work for Muslims who wish to attend Friday Prayers?

Laborde considers the issue of non-working days as it arises in societies with a Christian heritage and in which Sunday's being the traditional non-working day is no accident. However, many of those societies are now commonly described, including by Laborde (p. 232), as *post*-Christian and that raises another question: for how long must a society remain in thrall to its history? If the proportion of the population that regularly attends a Christian church on Sundays dwindles beyond a certain point, does the charge of 'majority bias' still stand? Is there a point at which Christians become merely chance-beneficiaries of the past rather than beneficiaries of contemporary bias? Has that point been reached already in the United Kingdom, given that only around 5% of the population regularly attends a Christian church on Sundays? Or can a society never escape its past? If the origins of Sunday as a non-working day lie with Christianity, does that suffice to make the traditional day of rest in post-Christian societies forever 'biased', even if, in the course of time, no-one remains a Christian? In a society like the United Kingdom, these questions are further complicated by the increasing use of Sunday as a working day and by courts' upholding the right of employers to refuse to accommodate the claims of Christian Sabbatarians.[6]

Aside from the complications specific to the case of non-working days, a group incurs a more general hazard, which Laborde notices (p. 231), if it rests its case for an exemption only on a claim of distributive unfairness. Consider again the case of the Tuesdayers and suppose that Saturdayers and the Sundayers complain that they are unfairly disadvantaged relative to Tuesdayers, a complaint that their society decides it should take seriously. It might remedy the unfairness by making Saturdays and Sundays protected non-working days for Saturdayers and Sundayers respectively. But it might also remove the unfairness by substituting Thursday for Tuesday as the society's non-working day, so that Tuesdayers become no less disadvantaged than other religious groups.[7] Indeed, given the costs and inconvenience of accommodating Saturdayers and the Sundayers, that substitution may well be the more attractive option. Religious groups are therefore well-advised to make disproportionate burden their primary claim to an exemption and to turn to a claim of bias only as an adjunct to that primary claim.

Notes

1. Unless otherwise indicated, page references are to Laborde, 2017.
2. Laborde sometimes writes as though coherence interests are unique to associations that are candidates for exemption. For example, she prefaces her inquiry into the types of association that are eligible for exemption with the simple question, 'which associations have coherence interests?', and goes on to argue that 'associations have coherence interests only if' they are both voluntary and identificatory associations (pp. 180–181). It is difficult to understand why an association that is involuntary or non-identificatory must be, for that reason, incapable of possessing coherence interests. Elsewhere, however, Laborde ascribes coherence interests to associations more generally (e.g. p. 178) and speaks of associations that have *pro tanto* claims to exemption as having 'the *relevant* coherence interests' and as exhibiting 'the *right kind* of coherence' (pp. 178, 182, 184, 185; my emphases). That, more intelligibly, implies that the coherence interests of associations differ in ways that bear on their eligibility for exemption. If, however, I have misunderstood the scope that Laborde means to give to the term 'coherence interest', that does not, I believe, affect what I say below about the substance of her argument.
3. For analysis and comment on the law now relating to who may and who may not discriminate on grounds of religion, including in respect of gender and sexual orientation, see Sandberg, 2011a, pp. 117–128, and Sandberg, 2011b, pp. 173–180.
4. E.g. *Reaney v. Hereford Diocesan Board of Finance* [2007] Employment Tribunal, judgement July 17 2007 (Case No.: 1602844/2006).
5. See, for example, the different views on those issues of Barry (2001, pp. 19–62) and Parekh (2006, pp. 239–263).
6. E.g. *Copsey v. WWB Devon Clays Ltd*, [2004] UKEAT/0438/03/SM; [2005] EWCA Civ 932 (a human rights case); *Mba v. The Mayor and Burgesses of the London Borough of Merton* [2012] UKEAT/0332/12/SM (an indirect discrimination case).
7. 'In 1829 the Ottoman Empire instituted a weekly day on which government offices were closed, and chose Thursday, which was a neutral day in terms of religious traditions' (Gavison & Perez, 2008, p. 204).

Acknowledgments

I am grateful to the participants in a UCL symposium on *Liberalism's Religion*, including Cécile Laborde, and to this journal's two anonymous referees, for their comments on an earlier version of this article.

Disclosure statement

No potential conflict of interest was reported by the author.

References

Barry, B. (2001). *Culture and equality*. Cambridge: Polity.
Bou-Habib, P. (2006). A theory of religious accommodation. *Journal of Applied Philosophy*, 23(1), 109–126.
Gavison, R., & Perez, N. (2008). Days of rest in multicultural societies: Private, public, separate? In P. Cane, C. Evans, & Z. Robinson (Eds.), *Law and religion in theoretical and historical context* (pp. 186–213). Cambridge: Cambridge University Press.
Jones, P. (1999). Beliefs and identities. In J. Horton & S. Mendus (Eds.), *Toleration, identity and difference* (pp. 65–86). London: Macmillan.
Jones, P. (2015). Toleration, religion and accommodation. *European Journal of Philosophy*, 23(3), 542–563.
Jones, P. (2017). Religious exemption and distributive justice. In C. Laborde & A. Bardon (Eds.), *Religion in liberal political philosophy* (pp. 163–176). Oxford: Oxford University Press.
Laborde, C. (2017). *Liberalism's religion*. Cambridge, MA: Harvard University Press.
Parekh, B. (2006). *Rethinking multiculturalism: Cultural diversity and political theory* (2nd ed.). Basingstoke: Palgrave Macmillan.
Sandberg, R. (2011a). *Law and Religion*. Cambridge: Cambridge University Press.
Sandberg, R. (2011b). The right to discriminate. *Ecclesiastical Law Journal*, 13(2), 157–181.

Religion and discrimination: extending the 'disaggregative approach'

Daniel Sabbagh

ABSTRACT
Cécile Laborde's disaggregation strategy, which is convincingly applied to religion, liberal neutrality, and freedom of association, should be extended to discrimination, in order to more systematically determine whether, when, and why indirect religious discrimination is unfair. Moreover, while Laborde's distinction between the 'Disproportionate Burden scenario' and the 'Majority Bias scenario' is a powerful alternative to the discrimination-focused account of the justifiability of religious exemptions, the epistemic status of that distinction is not immediately clear. A case can be made that Disproportionate Burden and Majority Bias do not map onto different *types* of minority exemption claims. They are *perspectives* or *analytical frames* that may jointly and usefully be applied to most instances of such claims.

As all groundbreaking works of scholarship, *Liberalism's Religion* is bound to attract comments from many angles. Mine will almost exclusively focus on the transversal issue of discrimination and the way in which it is addressed by Cécile Laborde. First, I will suggest that her disaggregation strategy, which is powerfully applied to religion, liberal neutrality, and freedom of association and that other political theorists have brought to bear on multiculturalism (Levy, 2000, chapter 5), can and should be more intensely applied to discrimination as well. Second, based on that disaggregation of the concept of discrimination, I will focus on two analytical connections between religion and discrimination and discuss their treatment in this book.

Disaggregating discrimination

As emphasized by Larry Alexander in a seminal article, 'discrimination is not one thing, but many' (Alexander, 1992, p 153). Despite the objections of a minority of political theorists (Young, 1990; within the frame of a purportedly radical perspective focused on the competing concept of 'oppression'; Cavanagh,

2002; within the frame of a libertarian perspective), since the 1970s discrimination has become 'an internally complex idea' (Laborde, 2017, p 9), less so than religion or liberalism, admittedly, but to an extent that does allow identifying 'an array of politically or legally relevant dimensions of' it (*id.*, 14). This is worth doing in connection with some of the arguments made by Laborde.

In *Liberalism's Religion*, discrimination – or rather the *direct* variety of discrimination – is classically understood as a differential treatment of individuals based on their membership in socially salient groups that potentially determines the allocation of scarce goods among them. According to the author of this definition, Kasper Lippert-Rasmussen, a group is 'socially salient' if 'perceived membership of it is important to the structure of social interactions across a wide range of social contexts' (Lippert-Rasmussen, 2014, p 30). Discrimination in this sense may or may not be legally banned, but when it is, the legal definition of it simply specifies the criteria according to which the 'socially salient groups' are defined. Thus, to take but one example, the European Union 2000 Race Directive indicates that 'direct discrimination shall be taken to occur where one person is treated less favourably than another is, has been or would be treated in a comparable situation on grounds of racial or ethnic origin' (European Union, 2000a).

At this point, two options are available. One can build injustice into the definition of discrimination so that it should only cover morally objectionable differential treatment (the *moralized* concept of discrimination); or, as Laborde does, one can settle for a morally neutral, non-evaluative definition of discrimination allowing for the possibility that it may be justified (the *descriptive* concept of discrimination) (see Singer, 1978, pp. 185–186). While the moralized concept of discrimination is increasingly widespread in the public sphere as a whole, the descriptive concept of discrimination still prevails within the community of moral philosophers, most of whom do not believe that discrimination is wrong per se.[1] It is also congruent with legal provisions such as South Africa's Bill of Rights inserted into the 1996 Constitution, according to which 'the state may not *unfairly* discriminate directly or indirectly against anyone on one or more grounds, including race, gender, sex, pregnancy, marital status, ethnic or social origin, colour, sexual orientation, age, disability, religion, conscience, belief, culture, language and birth' (Section 9, paragraph 3; emphasis mine). Obviously, the word 'unfairly' implies that, in some cases, discrimination can be fair.

The definitional issue is further complexified by the extension of the legal concept of discrimination that took place in the United States since 1971 (U. S. Supreme Court decision *Griggs v. Duke Power Company*, 401 U.S. 424 (1971)), in the United Kingdom since 1976 (Race Relations Act), and at the EU level since 2000 (European Union, 2000b), a concept that now encompasses *indirect discrimination* – in European terms – or disparate impact discrimination – in U.S. terms. 'Broadly speaking', on both sides of the Atlantic, indirect discrimination 'has three elements: equal treatment; a disproportionately exclusionary impact on those sharing a protected characteristic; and the absence of an acceptable justification' (Fredman, 2011, p. 154). While the rule or practice at stake does not entail differential treatment of individuals based on their membership in a group defined according to a 'forbidden ground' (Epstein, 1992) (1), it does have a disproportionately negative impact upon members of such a group (2), and it is not indispensable for the pursuit of a legitimate goal (3). Thus, under EU law, 'indirect discrimination shall be taken to occur where an apparently neutral provision, criterion or practice would put persons of a particular religion or belief (…) at a particular disadvantage compared with other persons, unless that provision, criterion or practice is objectively justified by a legitimate aim and the means of achieving that aim are appropriate and necessary' (European Union, 2000b). Conversely, if the aim is legitimate and if there is 'a reasonable relation of proportionality between means and aim' (*Abdulaziz et al. v. U.K.*, European Court of Human Rights, May 28 1985, paragraph 721), the fact that a given practice turns out to disadvantage members of a group defined by a 'forbidden ground' will not make it an instance of indirect discrimination.

However, on p. 261 (note 37), Laborde (2017) describes 'indirect discrimination that incidentally burdens religious believers' as 'permissible'. That statement is not entirely clear. Does she mean that, in some cases, a *legally* prohibited instance of 'indirect discrimination' may nonetheless be *morally* permissible? If so, examples of that disconnection between legal and moral acceptability as far as religion-based discrimination is concerned would have been helpful. Or does her endorsement of the descriptive concept of discrimination lead her to simply ignore the dissonant fact that the *legal* concept of *indirect* discrimination incorporates the lack of an acceptable justification? The sentence quoted above would then reflect her implicit reliance on an alternative, substantially broader understanding of indirect discrimination as encompassing any practice with an adverse impact on a religious minority, regardless of whether a defensible justification for the existence of that practice has been provided. Yet the choice of dismissing the legal definition of indirect discrimination sits uneasily with the extent to which Laborde uses legal cases to illustrate some of her key analytical distinctions. That tension is all the more noticeable as her main arguments are presented in part as an alternative to the competing theories of legal scholars such as Christopher Eisgruber, Lawrence Sager, and Andrew Koppelman – some of whom are also major contributors to the literature on antidiscrimination law (Koppelman, 1996). From the point of view of a reader familiar with this literature, instrumental references to legal decisions coupled with an unacknowledged rejection of key legal concepts are somewhat perplexing. Arguably, the transdisciplinary appeal of Laborde's book would have been increased by making explicit her departure from prevailing legal terminology as far as indirect discrimination is concerned.

Moreover, should one accept, for extra-legal, analytical purposes, Laborde's legally unorthodox conception of indirect discrimination, the central question involves the definition of the criteria based on which an instance of (direct or indirect) discrimination will be considered 'unfair' (Laborde, 2017, p. 54) or 'invidious' (*id.*) and therefore impermissible, a question that is not addressed in the book as forthrightly as one might have wished.

To address it, it is worth emphasizing that neither direct nor indirect discrimination as defined above make any reference to intent. Both may be either intentional or involuntary. While instances of direct and intentional discrimination – such as posting a sign 'No black need apply' on the door of a recruiter's office – are what most people have in mind when they think about direct discrimination, a sizeable and convincing literature in social psychology has established that acts of direct discrimination can be unconscious (for an overview, see Hamilton Krieger, 1995). An individual may well treat differently – and worse – members of a given group without being aware of doing so. In addition, *indirect* discrimination may be *intentional*: among U.S. examples, consider the so-called 'Grandfather Clauses' used by Southern states in the post-Reconstruction era to deprive blacks from their voting rights, or the array of 'apparently neutral' measures set up in order to reduce the proportion of Jews in the student body of Ivy League universities in the 1920s (Karabel, 2005; Oren, 1985; Synnott, 1979). Potential cases of discrimination can therefore be placed in a four-cell matrix including the following categories: direct and intentional discrimination; direct and unconscious discrimination; indirect and intentional discrimination; indirect and involuntary discrimination.

With this (admittedly rudimentary) typology in mind, is indirect religious discrimination unfair only when it is intentional (or specifically related to the decision maker's main purpose), as Laborde may seem to suggest by describing as 'permissible' 'indirect discrimination that *incidentally* burdens religious believers' (Laborde, 2017, p. 261, note 37 (emphasis mine))? Is discrimination unfair insofar as it would intentionally target a given religious group for disadvantage (whether that targeting is explicit – as in direct and intentional discrimination – or implicit – as in indirect and intentional discrimination)? Some thought-provoking arguments have been made by Deborah Hellman against this *intent-focused* or *purpose-focused* account of the wrongness of discrimination, in favour of a *meaning-focused* one, according to which the relevant question would be: does the discrimination under scrutiny objectively convey a demeaning message infringing on the dignity of the person discriminated against? (Hellman, 2008, chapter 6). Even though they are centred on race- and gender-based discrimination and not religious discrimination, those arguments are not obviously irrelevant to the topic at hand, especially given the ongoing racialization of Muslims in Europe and in the United States (Adida, Laitin, & Valfort, 2016; Meer, 2013). Yet they are not taken into consideration in *Liberalism's Religion*. Nor is the view that the observed disparate impact of a given practice may be unfair to the extent that it perpetuates the 'harmful effects' of past 'deliberate exclusion' (Wasserman, 1998, p. 811). Are the only groups that should be protected from (intentional or unintentional) indirect discrimination those that suffered direct and intentional discrimination in the past and that are negatively affected by the 'apparently neutral practice' at least in part as a consequence of that former discrimination of a different kind? In a nutshell, is unfair 'indirect discrimination (...) parasitic on [intentional] direct discrimination in that the latter requires the (*past*) presence of the former' (Lippert-Rasmussen, 2014, p. 17 (emphasis mine))? As far as religion is concerned, Laborde fails to consider this alternative understanding of the unfairness of indirect discrimination.

In a nutshell, to the extent that the author intends to provide normative guidance as to the permissibility of rules or practices inflicting a specific cost on individuals identified by their membership in a religious group, one might reasonably expect her to either precisely locate the criterion or criteria based on which fair and unfair religious discrimination may be distinguished from one another or, in a more radical vein, make an explicit case against the very notion of 'religious discrimination' (see Calvès, 2011), at least for philosophical – as opposed to legal – purposes. Yet Laborde does not clearly settle for one of those two mutually exclusive options.

Religion and discrimination: two analytical connections

Moving closer to the set of issues that the author *does* convincingly address, I will now consider two links between religion and discrimination.

The first one is encapsulated in the 'Ministerial Exception' of U.S. law, namely the notion that 'religious entities' are rightly 'exempt from regulation of their employment relation with their ministers [and, possibly, with other employees, too, depending on the religious dimension of the function they perform], including when the latter bring suits of discrimination on grounds of gender or sexuality' (Laborde, 2017, p. 57). In that case, religion is the ground upon which an exceptional freedom to discriminate is legally granted; it delineates a domain within which the antidiscrimination principle does not apply.

Laborde's treatment of this topic raises at least two questions which, considered jointly, lead me to wonder whether her stance vis-à-vis such exemptions is not overly deferential.

The first one arises in connection with the following sentence, which apparently summarizes her view on the matter: 'When discrimination is grounded in this way in religious doctrine – however objectionable the doctrine – courts should treat it as a case of permissible religious discrimination' (Laborde, 2017, p. 180). This assumes the possibility of providing an objective definition of the religious doctrine at stake at any given time. Yet surely there are cases in which the content of that religious doctrine is an object of intense controversy within the community of believers. In such cases, ultimately, where should the authority to decide what the genuine religious doctrine is and whether it requires discrimination be located? Laborde's answer is that the state, and courts in particular, should defer to pre-established religious entities: 'It is not for courts to force the church to change its doctrine: courts should respect the existing structures of authority within the church' (*id*.). Yet what about those cases in which the level of internal disagreement as to what the religious doctrine requires is high and the structure of religious authority is much more decentralized that in the case of the Catholic Church? Consider the hypothetical scenario in which a Muslim private school would lay off a female teacher based on her decision to stop wearing the hijab after having been hired? How should that case be addressed?

The second question revolves around Laborde's claim that 'the activities of a priest or a teacher of religion are relevantly religious, but not the activities of a janitor in a gymnasium – *there are obviously a wide range of intermediate functions and activities and associational "latitude for discrimination" should vary accordingly*' (Laborde, 2017, pp. 186–187 (emphasis mine)). Yet, even if there is some kind of continuum along which more or less religious functions or activities might be placed, at the end of the day a decision will have to be made as to whether to allow discrimination or not. As a practical matter, I fail to see how the extent of the discrimination allowed could be made proportional to the religious dimension of the practice at stake. Is it really possible to avoid a (more or less explicit) judgment as to whether the activity or function involved is 'relevantly religious' *enough* to authorize a potentially outcome-determining discrimination? Is the alternative here not a binary one, given the unavoidability of (at least implicitly) identifying the *discrimination-authorizing threshold of religiosity*? Appealing as it may be, this way of defusing or at least mitigating the ultimately political conflict between the competing principles of religious liberty and antidiscrimination strikes me as little more than a sleight of hand.

The second connection between religion and discrimination that I will briefly discuss springs from the claim that the lack of a religious exemption might be constitutive of an indirect and non-intentional discrimination, which may well be unfair despite its being both indirect and non-intentional. This is the claim made by Christopher Eisgruber and Lawrence Sager in their analysis of the U.S. Supreme Court decision *Sherbert v. Werner* (*Sherbert v. Werner*, 74 U.S. 398 (1963)). In this light, antidiscrimination would be the liberal rationale on the basis of which a religious exemption would be granted.

Laborde disagrees and offers her 'two-pronged theory' (Laborde, 2017, p. 214) based on the distinction between the 'Disproportionate Burden' 'scenario' (*id.*, 220) and the 'Majority Bias' scenario as an alternative to that discrimination-focused account of the justifiability of religious exemptions. Here is how those two scenarios are described:

'Disproportionate burden. Pursuit of some state regulatory interest makes it impossible for some citizens to fulfil an obligatory requirement of their faith of culture, yet makes it possible to relieve them of the burden without excessive cost. Disproportionate burden scenarios invite a *strict balancing test*, which weighs up the interest pursued by the law, the severity of the IPC [integrity-protecting commitment] burden, and the costs incurred in alleviating it. To illustrate: It would be unfair to compel Orthodox Jews to endure an invasive post-mortem autopsy in case of non-suspicious death, if they consider this a desecration of the body. There seems to be a *disproportion* between the aims pursued by the law and the burden it inflicts on the claimants.

Majority Bias. Minority citizens are unable to combine the pursuit of a core societal opportunity with an IPC, whereas the equivalent opportunity set is institutionally available to the majority. (...) To illustrate: it would be unfair to deny Muslims some time off on Fridays, as Christians can both go to Church on Sundays and hold a regular job' (id., notes omitted; author's emphasis).

This analytical distinction is both original and enlightening. Still, the vocabulary used to present it – the term 'scenario' in particular – may well be misleading. Arguably, Disproportionate Burden and Majority Bias are rather *dimensions* bound to be jointly present in a majority of cases. Would it not be possible, through some relatively basic shift in perspective, to redescribe most cases of Disproportionate Burden as cases of Majority Bias, and vice versa, which would then make it indeterminate whether any of such cases should instantiate the former or the latter?

Consider the illustration of a Majority Bias case given in the development quoted above. To use Laborde's own terms, why not settle for the following alternative description: Sunday closure laws do promote the legitimate 'state regulatory interest' of ensuring 'the temporal co-ordination of leisure time' (id., 148–149); yet, under a 'strict balancing test' this legitimate goal is not compelling enough to justify excluding devout Muslims from most employment opportunities, an exclusion that would qualify as a 'Disproportionate Burden'? Conversely, consider the example of the Newark Muslim Officers, a typical Disproportionate Burden case according to Laborde. In her view, their claim to be exempted from 'a regulation preventing them from wearing a beard on religious grounds' is a 'non-comparative' one that may be justified '*even in the absence of comparable medical exemptions*' (id., 57; author's emphasis). Yet, if one were to define the comparator differently – not as the group whose members share a health condition than prevent them from wearing a beard without experiencing unusual hardship, but as the group whose members are not subject to the religiously motivated prescription of beard-wearing –, would that case not recover its comparative dimension and arguably morph into one of Majority Bias? Consider the following thought experiment. Imagine all religions prescribe beard-wearing. In that case, how plausible is it that such a regulation would have been introduced? Insofar as it is implausible, this example is also one of Majority Bias. Laborde argues that, unlike Eisgruber and

Sager's approach of that case, hers has the advantage of 'avoid[ing] us having to search for hypothetical, presumptively advantaged non-religious comparator groups, in relation to which religious groups are discriminated against' (*id.*, 229). This is true. Yet searching for a presumably advantaged *religiously defined* comparator group, in relation to which Muslims are (indirectly and non-intentionally) discriminated against, would soon yield an obvious answer: arguably there is such a group as 'non-Muslims', and if that group did not exist, in all likelihood the rule the operation of which triggers the exemption claim would not exist either.

In short, a case can be made that the categories 'Disproportionate Burden' and 'Majority Bias' refer to *perspectives* or *analytical frames* that may be brought to bear on most cases of minority exemption claims, and not only to different *subsets* of such claims. In this light, the Disproportionate Burden perspective would focus on a comparative assessment of the costs and advantages of the rule under scrutiny, while the Majority Bias perspective would focus on the extent to which the genesis of that rule might have been impermissibly tainted by some background unfairness that would contaminate the effects of its operation. Granted, Laborde notes that 'many exemptions for minority members can be justified under either the disproportionate burden or the majority bias principle, or both' (*id.*, 235). Yet this acknowledgement appears only at the very end of the last chapter, seemingly as an after-thought. The same goes for the emphasis on the fraction of cases for which the distinction is the most crucial, namely those in which exemption claims can be made *only* on the basis of Disproportionate Burden, either because no comparator is available or because the group making the claim does not qualify as a minority (under the disputable assumption that the 'majority' referred to by the phrase 'Majority Bias' can be defined independently of the specific circumstances of the cases at hand and that this single definition is equally relevant across cases and operates as a fixed reference point). Again, this emphasis appears at the very end of the text (*id.*, p. 236), after the reader has been left wondering as to the epistemic status of the distinction between Disproportionate Burden and Majority Bias for some time.

Those are relatively peripheral comments, to be sure. This reflects in part my own limitations, but also how strong *Liberalism's Religion* is in the defence of its more central claims.[2]

Notes

1. This view is shared by Peter Singer (1978), Deborah Hellman (2008), Kasper Lippert-Rasmussen (2014), Thomas Scanlon (2008, p. 72-74), Mathias Risse and Richard Zeckhauser (2004), and Benjamin Eidelson (2015), *inter alia*, beyond their disagreements as to what makes discrimination wrong when it is.

2. I am grateful to the two anonymous reviewers selected by the *Critical Review of International Social and Political Philosophy* for generous and insightful comments on a previous version of this paper.

Disclosure statement

No potential conflict of interest was reported by the author.

References

Adida, C., Laitin, D., & Valfort, M.-A. (2016). *Why muslim integration fails in christian heritage societies*. Cambridge (Mass.): Harvard University Press.
Alexander, L. (1992). What makes wrongful discrimination wrong? Biases, preferences, stereotypes, and proxies. *University of Pennsylvania Law Review, 14*(1), 151–219.
Calvès, G. (2011). Les discriminations fondées sur la religion: Quelques remarques sceptiques. In E. Lambert Abdelgawad & T. Rambaud (eds.), *Analyse comparée des discriminations religieuses en Europe* (pp. 9–23). Paris: Société de législation comparée.
Cavanagh, M. (2002). *Against equality of opportunity*. Oxford: Clarendon Press.
Eidelson, B. (2015). *Discrimination and disrespect*. Oxford: Oxford University Press.
Epstein, R. (1992). *Forbidden grounds. The case against the employment discrimination laws*. Cambridge (Mass.): Harvard University Press.
European Union, 2000a. Council Directive 2000/43/EC of 29 June 2000 implementing the principle of equal treatment between persons irrespective of racial or ethnic origin
European Union, 2000b. Council Directive 2000/78/EC of 27 November 2000 establishing a general framework for equal treatment in employment and occupation.
Fredman, S. (2011). *Discrimination Law*. Oxford: Oxford University Press.
Hamilton Krieger, L. (1995). The content of our categories: A cognitive bias approach on discrimination and equal employment opportunity. *Stanford Law Review, 47*(6), 1161–1248.
Hellman, D. (2008). *When is discrimination wrong?* Cambridge (Mass.): Harvard University Press.
Karabel, J. (2005). *The chosen. The real story of admissions at Harvard, Yale, and Princeton*. Boston: Houghton Mifflin.

Koppelman, A. (1996). *Antidiscrimination law and social equality*. New Haven: Yale University Press.
Laborde, C. (2017). *Liberalism's religion*. Cambridge (Mass.): Harvard University Press.
Levy, J. (2000). *The multiculturalism of fear*. Oxford: Oxford University Press.
Lippert-Rasmussen, K. (2014). *Born free and equal? A philosophical inquiry into the nature of discrimination*. Oxford: Oxford University Press.
Meer, N. (ed.). (2013). *Racialization and religion*. New York: Routledge.
Oren, D. (1985). *Joining the Club. A history of Jews and Yale*. New Haven: Yale University Press.
Risse, M., & Zeckhauser, R. (2004). Racial profiling. *Philosophy and Public Affairs, 32*(2), 131–170.
Scanlon, T. (2008). *Moral dimensions. permissibility, meaning, blame*. Cambridge (Mass.): Harvard University Press.
Singer, P. (1978). Is racial discrimination arbitrary? *Philosophia, 8*(23), 185–203.
Synnott, M. G. (1979). *The half-opened door. discrimination and admissions at Harvard, Yale, and Princeton, 1900-1970*. Westport: Greenwood.
Wasserman, D. (1998). Discrimination: Concept of. In R. Chadwick (ed.), *Encyclopedia of Ethics* (pp. 805–814). San Diego: Academic Press.
Young, I. M. (1990). *Justice and the politics of difference*. Princeton: Princeton University Press.

Three cheers for liberal modesty

Cécile Laborde

ABSTRACT
Many liberals have been immodest in postulating that their own progressive, secular liberalism is the only one that can be justified in public reason. In *Liberalism's Religion*, I articulate a more modest theory of liberalism and religion. While I personally endorse progressive secular liberalism, I argue that it is only one of the reasonable conceptions of liberal justice. This liberal modesty has profound, hitherto unnoticed implications for (i) the role of religious arguments in the public sphere, (ii) the legitimacy of religious establishment, and (iii) the justifiability of religious exemptions. In this article, I defend these three claims by providing replies to my critics.

In current controversies about the place of religion in the state, liberal political philosophers tend to defend a progressive, individualistic, secular liberalism. Many of them, however, are also *political* liberals: they believe that liberalism is not the sectarian creed of left-wing progressives, and that it must be justified to all reasonable citizens. But these liberals have not considered whether alternative conceptions of the place of religion in the state can also be justified. Can there be reasonable disagreement about the place of religion in the state? Liberals have been immodest in postulating that their own progressive, secular liberalism also happens to be the only one that can be justified to all reasonable citizens. In *Liberalism's Religion*, I articulate a more modest theory of liberalism and religion. Although I personally endorse a version of progressive secular liberalism, I locate it among a broader set of reasonable conceptions of liberal justice.

Many liberal egalitarians argue that liberal neutrality demands (i) strict separation between state and religion (ii) no special treatment (e.g. exemptions) for religion. I deny both. I argue that while these commitments are compatible with liberalism, they are not entailed by it. There is greater reasonable disagreement about religion and the state than many liberals have thus far recognised. States meet liberal standards of legitimacy, in my view, when they implement one of the reasonable conceptions of liberal justice. The upshot is that liberals should not confuse their preferred conception of justice with the only reasonable one. Connectedly, they should not castigate as equally unreasonable conservative religious believers, on the one hand, and religious fanatics and fundamentalists, on the other. Not all critics of progressive, secular liberalism are unreasonable. Liberals' claims otherwise have fostered a disdainful and often vindictive alienation from liberalism on the part of many conservative religious believers. This is regrettable and dangerous (politically) and it is unsound (philosophically), as it goes against the spirit of Rawlsian political liberalism: to find mutual terms of cooperation among people who disagree profoundly, including about justice.

In what follows, I develop arguments for these various claims by providing responses to my critics in this volume. The majority of them cast doubt on my suggestion that secular, progressive liberalism is not the only reasonable conception of liberal justice. They focus their attention on three of my claims. The first is that public reason need not be substantively liberal; it only needs to be accessible. The second is that some forms of religious establishment are compatible with liberalism. The third is that neutrality is not incompatible with substantive judgements of integrity, which itself ground claims for exemptions. I explicate these three ideas in turn, and in the process make good on my defense of liberal modesty.

Public reason and accessibility

In Rawlsian versions of public reason liberalism, citizens appeal to shared liberal principles in their democratic deliberations. This is because, on a liberal conception of political justification, state coercion is legitimate when it appeals to reasons that reasonable citizens could accept. In *Liberalism's Religion*, I put forward a different conception of the relationship between public reason and liberal legitimacy. Instead of building liberal principles directly into the reasons that idealised citizens accept, I distinguish between public reason *stricto sensu* (the actual reasons that are the currency of democratic deliberation) and overall liberal legitimacy (the all-considered judgements about the liberal permissibility of institutions and laws). As a result, my theory of public reason is more permissive than Rawlsian versions: it draws on a broader pool of reasons than liberal principles of freedom and equality. My theory of liberal legitimacy, in turn, is more critical of existing practices: because it is not tied to already liberal societies, it provides external criteria with which to assess the legitimacy of laws and institutions in non-liberal societies. The upshot is that public reason *stricto sensu* is a necessary but not a sufficient condition for liberal legitimacy. A simple illustration suffices to make the point. A state may offer sound public reasons for its policies, yet these policies may be illiberal (consider, e.g. a state that justifies severe repressive policies by appeal to the notion of public order). My approach gives theoretical shape to this intuitive notion.

My critics in this volume focus on public reason *stricto sensu*, which I define as a principle of *public accessibility of state-proffered reasons*. Only reasons provided by state officials must be public: citizens may bring to democratic debate any consideration or argument they think is relevant to the issue at stake. State officials, by contrast, are under a duty to offer publicly accessible reasons when they seek to justify state coercion. It is not sufficient that reasons be *intelligible* only by reference to the standards of the speaker; but it is too demanding to require that reasons be *shared*: that all endorse the same reasons by reference to shared standards. Public reasons should, however, be *accessible*: they should be understood by actual citizens. Public reasons are the currency of democratic debate: when state officials present reasons for laws, it is important that citizens – even if they disagree with the law, or the reason – be able to assess and challenge them. On my theory, accessible reasons do not overlap with secular reasons: reasons can be inaccessible even if they are not religious, and not all religious reasons are inaccessible.

In his thoughtful commentary, **Sune Laegaard** presses me on the accessibility condition. How do we identify accessible reasons? Are reasons accessible when deliberators share the same premises or evaluative framework, even as they disagree about the validity of the reason? Or are reasons accessible when deliberators agree about the validity of the reason, yet disagree about whether it is sufficient to justify laws? The gist of Laegaard's comments is that it is more productive to conceptualise the accessibility of public reasons in relation to the latter ('output') than the former ('input') condition. He is right, and his useful suggestions allow me to reformulate the accessibility condition more precisely. On reflection, I should not have followed Vallier and D'Agostino in explicating accessibility by reference to shared premises (Vallier & D'Agostino, 2014). This condition is too demanding, and threatens to collapse accessibility into shareability, as Laegaard points out. Instead, let me say that accessible reasons are understood by citizens by reference *to their own or to shared premises*, and there is reasonable disagreement about whether they suffice to justify laws. (By contrast, intelligible reasons are understood only from the premises of the speaker, and they are not sufficient to justify laws. Shared reasons are understood from shared premises, and they are sufficient to justify laws).

Equipped with this slightly revised conception of accessibility, I now move to offer a response to **Aurélia Bardon**'s probing challenge. Bardon thinks that the accessibility condition is so weak that it fails to do any justificatory work. In controversies such that over same-sex marriage, my approach would unconvincingly distinguish between accessible reasons (such as appeal to the value of tradition) and non-accessible reasons (such as appeal to Biblical authority). Admittedly, the fact that a reason is accessible does not mean that it is a good or decisive reason; nor that is sufficient to legitimate particular laws. Bardon concedes this, yet she doubts that appeal to the value of tradition (*Tradition*) is any more accessible than appeal to Biblical authority (*Bible*). The accessibility condition cannot distinguish between them.

I disagree. To see why, let me distinguish three distinct types of reason. The first is appeal to divine authority, for example as revealed in the Bible. This is an intelligible reason (it can be understood by reference to the theistic premise of the speaker) but it is not accessible (one cannot disagree about what God wills without sharing the contested premise that God exists). The second is appeal to the value of tradition. Just like appeal to other contested values such as progress, welfare, sustainability, solidarity and so forth, it is accessible in my sense. This is because it *can be understood and endorsed from different premises, although there is reasonable disagreement about whether it suffices to justify laws*. For a reason to be accessible, it does not need to be grounded in shared premises, nor to be evaluated via a shared framework. It simply needs to figure in the set of reasons that have *some* weight in different evaluative frameworks. Such reasons are 'detachable' from specific evaluative frameworks, and state officials should not invoke the latter when advancing public reasons. C*ontra* Bardon's suggestion, this does not mean that deliberation about them is not possible, from a variety of comprehensive evaluative frameworks, in the public and private sphere. The key point Is that (*Tradition*) is accessible because it is detachable from particular comprehensive frameworks. (Different evaluative frameworks – perhaps barring revolutionary utopias – place some value on tradition, albeit for different deeper reasons: from the importance of legal stability and the honouring of legitimate expectations, to more conservative commitments to the intrinsic value of accumulated collective wisdom). By contrast, (*Bible*) is not accessible because it is not so detachable from a particular theistic framework.

The third type of reason is appeal to a secularized religious tradition, such as Christian (or Islamic, or Hindu) cultural tradition. This is also an accessible reason. What does the justificatory work is not appeal to deeper foundations such as divine authority, as in (*Bible*) but, rather, the empirically ascertainable embeddedness of Christianity in laws, norms and cultures. The fact that a particular cultural norm or practice has a religious origin does not make the authority of that norm inaccessible. Religious tradition, from this point of view, is no different from other kinds of tradition; and Christianity stands alongside Roman law or the Enlightenment as one among the variegated cultural sources of the western heritage. Just as we disagree about the continuing validity of Roman law or enlightenment rationalism, so we disagree about the validity of Christian-inspired ethical universalism or family law. The value of the patrimonial dimensions of religion can be debated even by those who deny that God exists and that he has made his Will known through a sacred text.

The upshot is this. (*Tradition*) might be a bad or unconvincing reason – I agree with Bardon that it often is. But it is not an invalid *qua* inaccessible reason. This is important in relation to controversies such as same-sex marriage. Conservative appeals to the value of the traditional family are *not* on the same plane, epistemically speaking, as appeal to Biblical authority. To suggest that they are is drastically to narrow public debate and confirm conservative suspicion that appeal to liberal public reason only serves to validate left-wing progressive legislation. Instead, liberals should say that while there may be *some* value in tradition, it is not sufficient to justify refusal to extend marriage to same-sex couples. On my view, the tradition-based rejection of same-sex marriage is deeply flawed, but this is not because it relies on epistemically suspect, non-public reasons. It is, rather, because it conflicts with liberal norms of equality and it is rooted in an unattractive vision of the good of marriage (Laborde, 2018).

While Bardon thinks accessibility is not sufficient, **Jeff Howard** contends that it is not even necessary for public justification. His argument is that if a law is unjust, the reasons given for it are irrelevant. Persecution of a gay citizen is unjust, regardless of whether it is undertaken by appeal to divine revelation or to accessible (if flawed) reasons. As Howard vividly puts it, it's all injustice to him.

I agree that the accessibility of justificatory reasons is not the only or the chief determinant of the justice of laws. Yet it does not follow that reasons are altogether irrelevant. It *does* matter whether the gay citizen is persecuted in the name of reasons that he – and the broader democratic public – can engage with. Persecution in the name of a faith that one does not share, just as oppression at the hands of an arbitrary and Kafkaesque power, adds the insult of epistemic alienation to the injury of unjust treatment. This, I think, is a plausible interpretation of the early modern insight that one of the most grievous wrongs of religious establishment is the fact that the state coerced citizens in the name of *faith* – a source not only of foundational disagreement but also of epistemic exclusion (Forst, 2011). The persecuted gay citizen may well object to (*Tradition*) as much as to (*Bible*); but at least (*Tradition*) can be contested and subjected to democratic deliberation.

To see the implausibility of Howard's suggestion, consider now a Christian state committed to liberal principles, which scrupulously upholds citizens' rights to freedom and equality, *because this is what the Bible demands*. If we grant Howard's view that the reasons for law are irrelevant to their legitimacy, this state is legitimate. But this is implausible. The problem with the Christian liberal state, on my view, is that it does not respect its citizens as democratic reasoners. It does not provide them with accessible reasons, as it makes the liberal quality of laws dependent on an interpretation of what the Bible demands. Only a sub-set of citizens, those for whom Biblical injunctions are normative, can engage in continuing democratic deliberation over what liberal principles of freedom and equality require. Accessibility turns out to be a necessary, separate condition.

Legitimacy, justice and religious establishment

In his wide-ranging challenge, Howard also puts pressure on the distinction I draw between legitimacy and justice. He agrees that *Divinitia* is legitimate but, in his view, this is not because it implements a reasonable conception of liberal justice. Rather, *Divinitia* is what Rawls calls a decent state: it is not fully liberal, but it is not so unjust that it forfeits its legitimacy. My own view is different. *Divinitia* does not implement my preferred conception of liberal justice, but it is a *bona fide* member of the family of reasonable conceptions of liberal justice. What Howard calls justice is *his* preferred conception of justice: the one he sincerely thinks is the best one. What I call justice is a broader set that includes my preferred conception of justice as well as other reasonable liberal conceptions of justice. While the difference might appear merely semantic, there are substantive issues at stake here.

First, I argue that the features that disqualify religious establishment at the bar of (any reasonable conception of) liberal justice are not present in *Divinitia*. Howard does not discuss them in detail, but it is significant that the objections he mounts against establishment in general are only valid against illegitimate forms of religious establishment – and therefore not against *Divinitia*. Howard objects to the state 'affirming truth' or endorsing 'divisive identities'. But this misses my point, which is that when religion is unconcerned with truth, or untainted by divisiveness, the reasons for objecting to its recognition by the state disappear. Recognition of religion, in these cases, is *permitted* by justice. It is not clear whether Howard disagrees.

Consider the following example. Suppose the great majority of the population of society X identify with a religion and suppose, further, that this is a non–truth-based, non-exclusive and non-divisive religion (perhaps a version of Buddhism, Sufi Islam, traditional African religion or Confucianism). On Howard's strict disestablishmentarian position, state symbolic recognition of this shared heritage is unjust, and the state of X should, instead, endorse strictly secular symbols and references. Suppose however that in X, secular symbols are culturally alien, for example because they are associated with an imported, western tradition. This is not to suggest that the introduction of liberal *laws and norms* is a western imposition (even if it is, it might be a legitimate one). It is, rather, that, as far as symbols are concerned, there is no such thing as cultural neutrality. Once we give their due to the cultural dimensions of all forms of symbolism – secular as well as religious – it is reasonable to hold the view that symbolic state recognition of religion might be at least permitted by justice, in cases where it is as (or more) inclusive than secular symbolism.

Second, to grant that proponents of *Divinitia* are reasonable entails that they have good reasons also to accept *Secularia* as a reasonable liberal state too. Consider, for example, debates about whether Muslims in Europe have good reasons to accept European secular orders. Can they be loyal to such states, not simply as a *modus-vivendi*, but as legitimate liberal orders? (March, 2009). My approach allows us to say that, while some Muslims might reasonably prefer a more religiously- friendly, *Divinitia*-style state, they have nonetheless good reasons to be loyal to *Secularia*. They may legitimately challenge the fairness of this or that particular arrangement in European *Secularia* (for example, some secular policies in France, see Laborde, 2008). But, just as Muslim-majority countries can favour *Divinitia*-style arrangements, so secularised countries can legitimately favour *Secularia*-style arrangements. Such states are not illegitimate just because they do not implement the particular (reasonable) conceptions of justice favoured by some of its citizens. My approach, therefore, allows us to recast the debate between advocates and critics of European secularism by highlighting a wider scope of reasonable agreement between them – agreement about the boundaries of reasonable disagreement itself.

Jean Cohen, much like Howard, doubts that any form of state religious endorsement is compatible with liberalism. Like him, though, she underplays the importance of introducing a more interpretive – disaggregative – conception of religion in order to distinguish between legitimate and illegitimate endorsement. Cohen's comments bring to light much of what we agree upon – even though the devil, as she notes, is in the details. I agree with her that while path-dependent symbolic establishments might be acceptable at time t, they might lose legitimacy at time t + 1 when increased religious and ethical pluralism makes disestablishment the least divisive, and the most egalitarian, option. Furthermore, and in contrast to what she implies, I too think that a state that enshrines religion as a source of law, announces an official religion, and enforces its tenets in its courts or via religious courts is not ever legitimate by liberal lights. My theory of minimal secularism, with its criteria of accessibility, divisiveness and personal freedom, is explicitly designed to explain what is wrong with such a state.

But the key point here is that what matters is not the particularly *religious* nature of the doctrine thereby established. It is, rather, its contingent features of inaccessibility, comprehensiveness and divisiveness. Consider family law in many contemporary states. It bears traces of traditional monotheistic moral and social norms – typically, monogamy, patriarchy, heterosexuality, fidelity, social reproduction. How compatible these legal norms are with liberal principles should not be determined by reference to whether the norms are really 'religious' or 'secular'. Rather, whatever their historical origin, they should be assessed in relation to their compatibility with principles of accessibility, freedom and equality.

Because I do not think that an undifferentiated concept of 'religion' can meaningfully be set as the opposite of 'liberalism', I am more relaxed than Cohen about the porosity between religion-friendly cultural formations and liberal orders. Struggles for emancipation and social reform have historically been spurred by religious movements, often against the oppressive, divisive or inegalitarian tendencies of secular regimes. Consider, to name just a few, the Civil Rights struggle in the United States, Liberation Theology in Latin America, the *Solidarnosc* movement in Poland, Islamic reform movements during the Arab Spring, and religiously-inspired pacifism around the world. It seems to me that no general case can be made that 'all religious identities are divisive if politicized', as Cohen contends. Instead, we should attempt to identify which features of religion should not be mobilised by state power, when, and why, without postulating that religious identity is in itself more inimical to liberal legitimacy than, say, nationalism, ethnicity or secular comprehensive ideologies.

Cohen also zooms in on our disagreement over the question of sovereignty and the challenge of religious institutionalism. Although I have been inspired by her pioneering work on this subject, I put forward a slightly different interpretation of that challenge. Religious institutionalists take liberal egalitarians to task for disregarding religious autonomy and asserting the state's prerogative to allocate the respective sphere of competences of groups. The question is: is this a disagreement about justice, or is it a more fundamental disagreement about sovereignty and jurisdiction? Are critics challenging the particular way in which the line is drawn, or are they challenging the authority of the state in drawing the line in the first place? By contrast to Cohen, I argue that the challenge is best understood as a reasonable disagreement about justice, not jurisdiction.

My main argument, as she notes, is exegetical. I show that, at crucial junctures of their argument, religious institutionalists such as Steven Smith or Victor Muniz-Fraticelli step back from drawing the radical implications of their own suggestions. In particular, they explicitly refuse to claim that churches should be sovereign over what they take to be their own affairs – that they should have *Kompetenz-Kompetenz*. My suggestion is that we should take them at their own words. Unless they are prepared to defend an alternative political order – perhaps a form of neo-medieval, radically pluralist constitutionalism – we should accept to see them as bona fide interlocutors in the debate about the boundaries of liberal justice. As I suggested in my introduction, to accuse all critics of liberalism of being apologists of religious sovereignty – of being essentially anti-liberal – makes liberalism unnecessarily sectarian. It also papers over real difficulties with the theoretical structure of liberalism – notably the fact that its commitment to sovereignty cannot be merely defended by appeal to freedom, rights and neutrality.

Sune Laegaard also raises questions about the distinction between legitimacy and justice, and in particular about my solution to the Jurisdictional Boundary problem. In Chapter 5 of *Liberalism's Religion*, I argue that once a state secures liberal legitimacy, it has the meta-jurisdictional authority to settle questions of justice, including setting the boundary of religion itself. In particular, the state has the authority to delimit the proper competences of religious associations in its midst. Laegaard agrees with my argument that liberal neutralists have no easy answer to the Jurisdictional Boundary problem and that, ultimately, they must justify and defend state sovereignty. Yet Laegaard identifies a potential problem with my two-pronged solution. Can the legitimacy of a state be assessed *before* and *independently* of its setting the jurisdictional boundary? This might run into a regress problem akin to the democratic boundary problem: as legitimacy depends on boundary-setting, it cannot precede it.

In response, let me state that it is not the case that *any* boundary setting is compatible with liberal legitimacy. As I argue in *Liberalism's Religion*, core liberal rights protect religious individuals and groups from coercion and persecution motivated by animus. A state that would not adequately protect these basic rights of religion would be illegitimate. Disagreement about this is not reasonable: sovereignty does not authorize violations of basic rights: it is *constrained* by principles of freedom and equality. Of course, this line of argument assumes a kind of second-order reasonableness: it assumes that there is no reasonable disagreement about the scope of reasonable disagreement. Reasonable disagreement cannot run all the way down without threatening liberal justice itself. On this point, I agree with political liberals such as Rawls and Quong. But I also suggest that when liberal principles are inconclusive or indeterminate about particular laws, it is acceptable to resort to procedural – democratic – solutions. States have what European lawyers calls a 'margin of appreciation' to interpret the scope of rights. On my view, there can reasonable disagreement about how far they should ban or endorse religious symbols, how deeply they should apply non-discrimination norms within church internal life, how much or how little religious education they should provide in schools, how much they should delegate the running of public services to civil society associations. It is insofar as its policies remain within the domain of reasonable disagreement about liberal justice that Divinitia is legitimate.

In her penetrating essay, **Chiara Cordelli** raises a fundamental philosophical objection to Divinitia – a fairness objection to any kind of religious establishment. This is a version of the neutralist critique of perfectionism – a debate closely related to the themes of *Liberalism's Religion*. Cordelli begins by taking seriously my own argument, that forms of religious establishment might not be objectionably inaccessible, comprehensive, or divisive. But, she asks, might they not be unfair in other ways, which are not captured by my theory? Given that even symbolic establishment requires extraction and transfer of resources (typically, through taxation), how can we justify that some citizens be required to subsidize the conceptions of the good of others? Is this not *unfair*?

In response, let me first note that to be required to subsidise a policy that one disagrees with is not unfair. Right-wing libertarians are required to subsidise welfare states; and pacifists' taxes are channelled towards expensive defence budgets. One might reply that those disagreements are disagreements *about justice*, not about the good. But, then, the onus is on neutralists to explain why disagreements about justice are less egregious from the perspective of the justification of coercive taxation to dissenters. The most sophisticated argument is Quong's distinction between foundational and merely justificatory disagreement. But, as I show in Chapter 3 of *Liberalism's Religion*, the distinction is not plausible, and it has been convincingly rebutted by others (Fowler & Stemplowska, 2015). Neither appeal to the mere fact of disagreement, nor appeal to different types of disagreement helps explain why taxing in the name of the good is more unfair than taxing in the name of justice.

Cordelli anticipates this response, and points out that while a political order *has to* realise justice (it is a condition of its legitimacy) it does not *have to* endorse any conception of the good. So the question can be reformulated as follows: why is endorsement of the good permissible, given that it is not required? Critiques of neutralism have offered a variety of answers to this question. They have said, for example, that endorsement of the good is permissible when it is not paternalist – or otherwise disrespectful of people's abilities to find the good for themselves –; or when it is non-coercive; when it is merely aspirational instead of edificatory, and so forth (Kramer, 2017). For my part, I have suggested a three-criteria test for the legitimacy of religious endorsement (and, by extension, perfectionist policies). Appeal to the good has to be grounded in public, accessible reasons; the policy has to respect the equal status of all citizens; and the policy should not impose a comprehensive ethics of life on citizens. Properly interpreted, I believe that these criteria take the sting out of the neutralist challenge to perfectionism, including Cordelli's version of it. While most taxation for purposes of religious endorsement will be illegitimately unfair, some will be permissible.

I would concede a point to Cordelli, however. The fact that a policy of religious establishment is not *illegitimately unfair*, as I put it, does not mean that it is not unfair from the perspective of some reasonable conceptions of liberal justice. I do not deny, in particular, that the taxation of secular citizens for the maintenance of even purely symbolic religious establishment raises issues of justice. But, once we are satisfied that the policy meets the three criteria of minimal secularism, further debate about whether the policy is fair falls under the domain of reasonable democratic debate. The issue cannot be resolved directly by appeal to second-order neutrality (or secularism). As a citizen, I may hold that justice requires both an extensive, universal welfare state and a strictly secular state. But I should recognise that others may reasonably disagree with me – because they favour a libertarian state or a more religiously inspired state. In that case, I must be prepared to make my case in democratic deliberation and – were the majority to prefer a libertarian Divinitia – I must accept that it is not illegitimately unfair that I be taxed to support that state.

Cordelli further asks whether the fact that a state symbolically endorses integrity-protecting commitments (such as religion) rather than bare preferences (such as beer-drinking) does any work in this argument. It does not. I argue that some symbolic religious establishment might be permissible if it is endorsed democratically. But what makes it permissible is that it is endorsed democratically, not that it is religious. A democratic state could as legitimately choose to promote beer drinking (the municipality of Munich has funded the popular beer festival of *Oktoberfest* almost without interruption since 1819). So it is important to stress – contrary to Cordelli's interpretation – that the moral weight of integrity does not justify state special *support* for religion. If anything, the moral weight of integrity justifies greater restraint on the part of the state in interfering within the sphere of personal ethics (this is how I reconstruct Dworkin's version of restricted neutrality, which applies it primarily to religious and sexual ethics). When public authorities intervene in such areas, they are particularly prone to violate both personal liberty and civic equality, in precisely the ways that minimal secularism disallows. The upshot is that religious establishment is permissible if and only if it is as benign as a beer festival.

So the notion of integrity teaches a negative lesson from the point of view of what the state can permissibly *support*: it singles out those areas of life where state promotion is *prima facie* suspect. But the notion of integrity also has a positive import from the point of view of what the state has a duty to *protect*. It explains why freedom of religion and conscience are special liberties, which can only be limited – or burdened – by appeal to compelling state interests. The difference between state support and state protection is, of course, a contested one – it stands at the intersection of the Establishment and Free Exercise Clauses of the First Amendment and is at the heart of the most contested judicial decisions of the US Supreme Court. But it is, I think, one of our firmly considered judgements that a law that burdens religious exercise violates liberty to a greater extent than a law that burdens beer drinking, or any other bare preference. The notion of integrity – a weakly perfectionist notion – explains why this is true. It is still the case, as Cordelli insightfully remarks, that the difference between integrity-respecting commitments and bare preferences is not as clear as it could be. On this point, I readily concede that more work needs to be done.

Integrity, exemptions, discrimination

Paul Bou-Habib develops a different challenge to my conception of integrity. I have been inspired by his important writings on the subject, and we agree on most substantive judgements. But we take somewhat different argumentative paths. In previous work, Bou-Habib has argued that the normative force of claims for religious accommodation lies in the value of integrity – on this we agree. In his commentary, Bou-Habib sharply zooms in on the remaining differences between us. As he notes, our accounts are not likely to differ much in their practical implications. We agree that while it is necessary that claims for exemptions be justified by appeal to the integrity of the claimant, this is not sufficient. The pursuit of integrity must be constrained by the rights of others (and other interests pursued by the law). We might also reach identical substantive conclusions in a range of different cases.

We differ, however, in how we conceptualise the relationship between integrity and morality. The test I favour has three steps. It asks whether (i) the claimant's integrity is bound up with the practice (a non-moralised integrity test); (ii) the practice meets some minimal standards of moral acceptability (a moral abhorrence test) (iii) the practice is compatible with the publicly affirmed liberal conception of justice (an overall permissibility test). Bou-Habib's test, by contrast, has a simpler, two-stage structure: (i) does this practice show basic consideration for the rights of others (moralised integrity); and (ii) is it compatible with the interests pursued by the law (overall permissibility)?

My three-stage test has, I think, two main advantages. First, a non-moralised definition of integrity allows us to recognise that people can perform morally abhorrent actions with integrity. Consider actions performed in tragic situations, where agents must sacrifice something of value in order to pursue something else of value. The ethical dilemmas in which Abraham and Antigone found themselves are poignant because we recognise their tragic predicament. When Bou-Habib writes that there is no value in committing a morally abhorrent act, he means that we should not commit them. This may be true, but the formulation erases the crucial difference between doing something morally abhorrent out of brutality, hatred, or wickedness, and doing something abhorrent 'with regret' – in full awareness of one's morally compromised position. To illustrate, consider a parent with two critically ill infants. Both will die unless one of them donates his vital organs to the other. The parent might sacrifice one of her children (thereby doing something morally abhorrent) but this might be the only way for her to maintain her integrity (as a loving mother). Cases such as these suggest that we should not build moral acceptability into our definition of integrity. Some acts are morally abhorrent (and therefore should not be considered for exemptions) but they may still be compatible with integrity (and underpin extenuating circumstances judgements, for example).

The three-stage test has an additional, more significant advantage. It allows judges to treat a wide range of reasonable, non-morally abhorrent claims with appropriate respect. What I call morally ambivalent claims are claims that could be fitted into one of the reasonable conceptions of liberal justice. They, however, can be turned down *at the third stage* because they conflict with the rights of others, as interpreted through the publicly affirmed conception of liberal justice. To grant morally ambivalent claims stage-2 recognition – to see them as *pro tanto* candidates for exemption – is a way publicly to affirm the reasonableness of some disagreements about liberal justice. Bou-Habib's theory, by contrast, makes no space for the category of morally ambivalent claims. All the moral work is done at the first stage: either a practice shows 'consideration for the rights of others' – in which case it shows integrity, and goes through – or it doesn't – in which case it does not exhibit integrity in the first place, and gets rejected *on this ground*. One unfortunate implication is that morally abhorrent practices such as infant sacrifice are considered in exactly the same way as morally ambivalent practices such as mild corporal punishment inflicted on children. Bou-Habib claims that the difference does not amount to much if both these practices are denied exemptions at the last stage. But I think the stage of the deliberation during which the rejection happens matters, because it concerns the public affirmation of the moral status of the practice.

To illustrate, consider a parent (or a school with a traditionalist religious ethos) who sincerely believes that the moral edification of her child would benefit from occasional mild corporal punishment. On my three-step judgement, a judge might respond to the claim by saying 'Yes, your integrity is at stake; and no, this is not a morally abhorrent action. But we have an overriding commitment to protect the child's interest, so we will deny your claim.' By contrast, on Bou-Habib's moralised two-step judgement, the judge will in effect say: 'you have failed to show basic consideration for the interests of others; therefore you do not even act with integrity'. The problem with this response is two-fold. First, it does not take seriously the difference between the violent, wicked child-abuser and the conscientious traditionalist parents. It denies that the latter are reasonable, and that their conception of the good is not incompatible with one of the permissibly liberal conceptions of justice. Even worse, it denies that the traditionalist parents act with any kind of integrity. Bou-Habib's moralised theory would treat the claims of traditionalist believers who are reasonable in a political liberal sense in exactly the same way as it would treat unreasonable fanatics and wicked murderers. This, in my view, is the main flaw of the two-stage approach. It unconvincingly builds a sectarian conception of what it means to 'show consideration for the interests of others' into the notion of integrity. One implication is that only religious believers who act out in strict conformity with the publicly affirmed liberal conception of justice have any chance of obtaining an exemption. My theory, by contrast, allows for reasonable disagreement over what it means to treat others with basic consideration (above a minimal threshold of moral non-abhorrence).

Peter Jones also finds fault with my conception of integrity. His is a nuanced, thoughtful and wide-ranging critique. I shall focus on two fundamental points. First, Jones is not convinced by my attempt to substitute a theory of *integrity* for the simpler, conventional notion of freedom of *religion*. In his view, freedom of religion provides a straightforward rationale for both individual and collective cases of exemption. *Individuals* who seek exemptions seek to do what is right, because it is demanded by God: they are not primarily motivated by a wish to act out of integrity. Similarly, *groups* who seek religious exemptions merely seek to practice religion collectively: they are not primarily motivated by concerns about their associational integrity or coherence.

I do not deny that these are key dimensions of the religious experience. Phenomenologically, it seems highly plausible that religious believers, acting individually or collectively, do so out of a first-order commitment to do right by their faith, not out of a second-order commitment to act with integrity. But, the question we should ask, on the interpretive approach defended in *Liberalism's Religion*, is not: 'what is the religious experience like?' but, rather, 'what is it about the religious experience that generates specific duties on others?'. This is particularly salient in the case of exemptions, where what has to be justified is a special not a general right: a right not to be subjected to obligations that fall on others. The advantage of integrity, as pointed out by Bou-Habib, is that it appeals to a good that can be recognised as a good even by non-religious citizens. It is also more specific than a general interest in doing what is right – which, in itself, is too weak to justify a *pro tanto* right to exceptions. Integrity, in a word, picks out what is ethically salient in the religious experience when a claim to exemption is made – a value that is weighty enough to ground duties of others. But it is true, as Jones notes, that as individual believers themselves define what is central to their integrity, the individual integrity standard remains a subjectivist standard. This is, I think, an advantage of the integrity view: judges do not have to get embroiled in definitions of what is and what is not objectively 'religious', when what is at stake is the ability of individuals to live with integrity as they see it.

The standard of collective integrity, by contrast, is not purely subjective. While individuals have final sovereignty over which values and purposes are central to their integrity, it is not so clear, in the case of groups, who has the authority to define what collective integrity demands. It is not enough, for example, for the shareholders of *Hobby Lobby* to claim that their for-profit family business is 'religious' for the company to benefit from religious freedom protections. What matters, I argue, is a more objective test of integrity –

a test of coherence, for example, between the actual purposes of those joining the association and the activities it centrally pursues. Because granting exceptions to groups often means granting them special powers over their individual members (e.g. no protection from anti-discrimination legislation), group leaders cannot be the sole, sovereign adjudicators of collective integrity. The integrity of artificial collective persons, then, has a different shape from the integrity of natural persons.

The second important objection raised by Jones concerns the two justifications for individual exemptions that I put forward – Disproportionate Burden and Majority Bias. Jones casts doubt about the scope of the latter. How do we know, he asks, whether non-neutral social rules are objectionably *biased*? He raises two examples. First, Jews and Sabbatarians incidentally benefit from the recognition of Saturday as a day of rest in addition to Sunday (in post-Christian societies). On my theory, however, the mere presence of an advantage only constitutes majority bias if it benefits historical majorities. Second, are Christians still beneficiaries of the Sunday rule, given that the great majority of them do not go to church on Sundays? It is true that majority bias is eroded by societal secularization. Yet (for now) it persists, not necessarily through greater advantages and benefits, but in the complex modes of symbolic recognition of historically dominant identities. Muslims' demand for Friday exemptions make sense against a background of broader *cultural* dominance of historically Christian groups, and need not rigidly track the current distribution of opportunities for *religious* exercise between majority and minorities. That said, I share Jones's view that religious accommodation is often best defended from Disproportionate Burden rather than Majority Bias, as what counts as unfair background in religiously diverse, and mostly secularised societies is often difficult to tell.

Daniel Sabbagh takes up similar issues, and raises probing questions about my treatment of the notion of discrimination. He rightly notes that I do not systematically frame my analysis in terms of discrimination, that I use an implausibly non-moralised, descriptive conception, and that I make few references to actual discrimination law. I plead guilty to all these charges. But this is because I do not think that the legal notion of discrimination is the best analytical framework to theorize the fair accommodation of religious claims.

This, I should note, is not as eccentric a position *in law* as Sabbagh's critique might imply. A number of lawyers and legal theorists have expressed suspicion about the notion of religious discrimination (Calvès, 2011); and the accommodation of religious claims, in countries such as the United States and Canada, is not primarily driven by a discrimination framework. To be sure, the notion of discrimination is useful to capture the wrong of egregious types of disparate treatment that are motivated (or can only be justified) by anti-religious animus (or prejudice against racialized religious groups). But more problematic is the view that any law or rule that incidentally burdens some religious citizens is *prima facie* discriminatory, just because of the disparate burden it occasions. It is because I am sceptical about the scope of the notion of indirect religious discrimination that, in *Liberalism's Religion*, I try to articulate two alternative frameworks, which I call Disproportionate Burden and Majority Bias.

As Sabbagh notes, legal theorists such as Christopher Eisgruber and Lawrence Sager seek to ground the liberal justification for religious exemptions in ideals of equality and non-discrimination. It is because some religious groups are victims of structural prejudice and casual neglect that measures should be taken to rectify the disadvantage they suffer. On this view, members of religious minorities suffer discrimination, on a par with members of racial or sexual minorities. I endorse the egalitarian, discrimination-based argument for exemption (of which Majority Bias is a formulation) but I do not think it is always the best or most appropriate framework to scrutinize the fairness of religious accommodation.

First, the discrimination framework is too collectivist, and is unable to accommodate the individualization of religious freedom claims. In the UK *Eweida* case, adoption of a discrimination-based framework led judges to reject a British Airways employee's demand to wear a Christian cross, on the grounds that she belonged to no group that held it a duty to wear a cross. On my view, we should not ask whether Eweida is discriminated against as a member of a vulnerable group of Christians. Rather, we should ask whether the exercise of what she takes to be her religious duty is disproportionately burdened by the rule. The Disproportionate Burden test allows us to assess Eweida's claim on its own merits, without having to look for a broader disadvantaged group.

Second, and connectedly, the discrimination framework requires that an independent measure of group disadvantage be provided. Women or members of racial minorities are wrongly discriminated against by some facially neutral rule just in case the rule perpetuates or aggravates the disadvantage they *already* suffer. By analogy, one can say that members of religious minorities are disadvantaged by rules that accentuate existing institutional biases towards religious majorities. (This is captured by the Majority Bias test.) But it seems more problematic to say that religious citizens are discriminated against just by virtue of living under secular (non-religious) institutions. In post-Christian societies, Christians are *not* a religious minority in the way that Muslims or Jews are (although members of minority Christian groups, such as Sabbatarians in the United States, may be). This does not mean that members of historically dominant religions have no claim for exemption at all. It means that the claim they have falls under Disproportionate Burden, rather than Majority Bias. Disproportionate Burden is a more stringent, but also a more individualised test, as I suggested above. It is a test rooted in the value of religious freedom, not one rooted in the value of equality. Religious accommodation, in other words, is not only or always a response to wrongful discrimination. Religious identity is sometimes like race or gender and, in that case, should be protected by anti-discrimination measures; but at other times it should be treated as a first-person, integrity-protecting commitment – with less extensive protection. Analysis of the limits of the discrimination framework, then, brings out the need to work with a differentiated, disaggregated conception of religion, as I argue in *Liberalism's Religion*.

Acknowledgements

The author is grateful to Aurélia Bardon and Jeff Howard for their dedicated work in putting together this special issue.

Disclosure statement

No potential conflict of interest was reported by the author.

References

Calvès, G. (2011). Les discriminations fondées sur la religion: Quelques remarques sceptiques. In E. Lambert Abdelgawad & T. Rambaud (Eds.), *Analyse comparée des discriminations religieuses en Europe* (pp. 9–23). Paris: Société de Législation Comparée.
Forst, R. (2011). *Toleration in conflict. past and present*. Cambridge: Cambridge University Press.
Fowler, T., & Stemplowska, Z. (2015). The asymmetry objection rides again: On the nature and significance of justificatory disagreement. *Journal of Applied Philosophy, 32*(2), 133–146.
Kramer, M. (2017). *Liberalism with excellence*. Oxford: Oxford University Press.
Laborde, C. (2008). *Critical republicanism. The hijab controversy and political philosophy*. Oxford: Oxford University Press.
Laborde, C. (2017). *Liberalism's religion*. Cambridge Mass.: Harvard University Press.
Laborde, C. (2018). Abortion, marriage and cognate problems. *The American Journal Of Jurisprudence, 63*(1), 33–48. doi:10.1093/ajj/auy007
March, A. (2009). *Islam and liberal citizenship. The search for an overlapping consensus*. Oxford: Oxford University Press.
Vallier, K., & D'Agostino, F. (2014). 'Public Justification'. In Edward N. Zalta (Ed.), *The Stanford Encyclopedia of Philosophy*. Retrieved from http://plato.stanford.edu/archives/spr2014/entries/justification-public/

Index

Note: Page numbers followed by "n" denote endnotes.

accessibility condition 10–15
accessible premise 31–33, 34n7
accessible reasons 22, 41–43, 121
agent-relative perspective 14–15
agent's own standards 12
Alexander, Larry 109
Anglican Church, Great Britain 71–74, 77
anti-homosexual religious beliefs 91
anti-perfectionism 11
associations: coherence interests 63–64, 98–101, 107n2; competence interests 98, 101–103; justification of exemptions 99; religious associations 101

bad/unconvincing reason 123
Bardon, Aurélia 121–122
Bou-Habib, Paul 96, 130–132
British discrimination law 101–102

Calhoun, Cheshire 95
Catholic Church 5, 17, 73, 98, 100, 101–102
church autonomy 17, 62
civic inclusiveness 16–17
coercive laws 41
coercive state policies 69
Cohen, Jean L. 59, 65n3, 125–126
coherence interests, associations 63–64, 98–101, 107n2
collective integrity 132–133
collective religious exemptions 97–98
commitments 95
common justificatory framework 39, 46n5
common standards **11**, 12
competence interests, associations 98, 101–103

consensus positions 12
contemporary liberal-egalitarianism 72, 73–74
convergence positions 12
Cordelli, Chiara 127–129
critical religion challenge 48
critical religionists' approach 49–50

D'Agostino, F. 121
democratic boundary problem 127
democratic legitimacy 55
democratic reasoners 11, 23, 42
differentiation, spheres of society 49
disaggregation approach 4, 10, 51
disagreement 12
discrimination: definition 109–110; framework 134–135; indirect 111–112; intent-focused/purpose-focused account 112–113; intentional 112; legal concept 110–111; legally unorthodox conception, indirect discrimination 112; moralized concept 110
disproportionate burden 103–105, 114–116, 133, 134
Divinitia 43, 45, 53, 54, 56, 124
divisiveness 52
Dworkin, Ronald 2, 37, 40, 51, 70, 72

egalitarian theory, religion 2
Eisgruber, Christopher 2, 43, 114, 115, 134
empirical claims 13
empirical theory, public reason 16
enactment 90
epistemic claim 38
epistemic distinction 14–15
epistemic wrong 10, 23, 42
Equality Act (2010) 100, 102

INDEX

ethical claims 96
ethical commitments 95
ethical evaluations 70
ethical independence 70–71
ethical integrity 64
ethically salient commitments 76
European Union 2000 Race Directive 110
Eweida case 134
exclusively religious arguments 40–41, 46n7
exclusivist positions 11–12

fairness 72, 73–74

Galston, W. 92n1
Gaus, Gerald 11
Grandfather Clauses 112
Greenawalt, K. 92n1
Greene, Abner S. 60, 65n11

heterosexual couples 24
hierarchical account of autonomy 93n11
Hirschl, R. 52, 65n6
Hobby Lobby case 100
Howard, Jeff 123

identity-IPCs 6
identity-protecting commitment (IPC) 6
illegitimate endorsement 125
impersonal value 40
inclusiveness condition 15–17
inclusive state 43–45
inclusivist position 11–12
indirect discrimination 111–112
integrity: Jones's views 132; moralised account 84, 86–89, 92, 92n10; non-moralised accounts 82–84, 92; religious believers 81–82; religious convictions 83; responsiveness 89–92; theory of 132; valuable/respect-worthy conviction 85
integrity-protecting commitments 83, 95, 129
intelligibility condition 11–12
intelligible reasons 22, 122
intent-focused/purpose-focused account, discrimination 112
interpersonal liberal justice 50
IPC *see* identity-protecting commitment (IPC)

Jeremy 79
Jones, Peter 132–133
jurisdictional boundary problem 3, 4

justifiable state 41–43
justificatory disagreements 38–39
justificatory reasons 123

Kant, Immanuel 79
Kompetenz-Kompetenz 59, 126

Laborde, Cécile: accessibility, epistemic account of 22–25; agent-relative perspective 14–15; coercive laws 41–42; contemporary liberalism 71; critical religion challenge 48–49; disaggregation approach 10; egalitarian liberalism 51–52; hostility, liberal egalitarians 36; inclusivist/convergence positions 11–12; indirect discrimination 111–112; infant sacrifice 85–86, 90; integrity 95–97; integrity *vs.* identity 97; justificatory *vs.* foundational disagreement 38–39; liberal democratic state 53; liberal-egalitarian approach 3; liberal legitimacy 51; minimal secularism 21, 70; public justification 22–23, 25, 28; *vs.* Rawls 27; reason-relative perspective 14–15; religious exemption 95–97; state coercion 78–79
Laegaard, Sune 121, 126–127
The Law of Peoples (Rawls) 45
Laycock, Douglas 62
legitimate endorsement 125
liberal democracy 62
liberal democratic state 53
liberal egalitarian approach 2–3, 48, 58
liberal-egalitarian legitimacy 69–70
liberal-egalitarian societies 69
liberalism 51
Liberalism's Religion (Laborde, Cécile) 3, 9, 21, 36, 37, 48, 69, 94, 109, 110, 112, 119, 120, 126–128, 132, 134
Liberalism Without Perfection (Quong, Jonathan) 38
liberal justice 124
liberal legitimacy 120; accessibility 15; function of 18; of policies 11
liberal neutrality 69, 70
liberal non-theocratic state 57
liberal states: anti-perfectionist, state policies 69; full neutrality, majority and minority religions 69; qua religion 2; religion, treatment of 2; religious freedom 1
liberal theory of associational freedom 63
Lippert-Rasmussen, Kasper 110
Locke, John 68

INDEX

Maclure, J. 2
majority bias 105–107, 114–116, 133, 134
McConnell, Michel 65n11
Mein Kampf 42–43
Mele, A. 93n11
meta-jurisdictional authority 18–20
meta-jurisdictional sovereignty 17–20, 57, 58
mild corporate punishment 89
minimal epistemic validity 28
minimal liberal secularism 11
minimal secularism 51
ministerial exception, churches 63
moral authority 32
moral integrity 95
moralised account 84, 86–89, 92n10
morally abhorrent practices 131
moral/metaphysical premises: evaluation 29–30; shareability 30–31; source 31–33
Muniz-Fraticelli, Victor 60, 61, 65n11, 126

New Natural Law 42
non-accessible premise 31–33, 34n7
non-accessible reasons 4, 24
non-moralised accounts 82–86
normative claim 38
notion of discrimination 133–134
Nussbaum, M. 43

obligation-IPCs 6
Orthodox Jews 81–82

pace prevailing wisdom 36
paternalistic policies 38, 45n3
Patten, Alan 73
perfectionist policies 38
permissibility pool 42
permissible religious discrimination 113–114
personal ethics 40
political liberalism 37–39, 65n9
political liberals 119–120
political secularism 65n3
public accessibility, state-proffered reasons 121
public assessment 27
public justification 43, 46–47n10
public reason 11, 13–16, 23, 28, 41, 78, 120–121

Quong, Jonathan 12, 37–39, 45n1, 60, 78–79, 127
Quong's theory 38

Rand, Aynd 76
Rawls, John 2, 27, 72, 73, 79n2, 124, 127
Raz, Joseph 39
reasonable disagreement 20, 38–39, 88–89, 127
reasonableness 23, 34n4
reason-relative perspective 14–15
reciprocity 79
religion-friendly cultural formations 125–126
religious associations 98, 101
religious believers, integrity 81–82
religious commitments 81–82
religious discrimination 113–116
religious establishment: inclusive state 43–45; justifiable state 41–43; religion in, public life 40–41
religious exemption 95–97
religious freedom: intrinsic religious goods 2–3; liberal states 1; religion, treatment of 2
religious institutionalism 50
religious minorities 44
religious symbols 54
republican approach, institutional design 44
restricted neutrality 39
restricted *vs.* broad neutrality: impersonal value 40; personal ethics 40; political liberalism 37–39; reasonable disagreement 38–39
right-wing libertarians 128
rules of logic 27
rules of reasoning 27–29
rules of science 27

Sabbagh, Daniel 133–135
Sager, Lawrence 2, 43, 114, 116, 134
same-sex marriage 24–27, 121–123
Schragger, R. 50, 61
Schwartzman, M. 50, 61
second moral power 38
Secularia 56, 124–125
secularized religious tradition 122
secular liberalism 59
self-binding 46n5
self-determination 77
separation, religious establishment: accessible reasons 71–72; church and state 17–18; demanded by justice 74–75; ethical independence 70; ethically salient matters *vs.* mere preferences 75–76; fairness 72, 73–74; 'internal' integrity-based

criterion 76; publicly acceptable criterion 76; reciprocity 79; self-determination 77; social identity, marker of vulnerability 71; unfair policies of establishment 72–73
shareability condition 11–13
shareable reasons 22
Smith, Steven D. 60, 61, 65n11, 126
social cohesion 16
South Africa's Bill of Rights 110
standards of evaluation 26–27
state authority, theory 39
state endorsements 52
state neutrality 2; accessible reasons 71–72; ethical independence 70–71; social identity, marker of vulnerability 71
state secularism 60
state sovereignty 17, 18, 58–59
subjective theory, religious freedom 86–88

substantive distinction 14–15
substantive wrong 23, 24, 34n5
symbolic establishment 16, 54

Taylor, C. 2
thick sincerity test 6, 83, 84, 92n5
thin acceptability 6, 92n5
three-stage test, integrity and morality 130–131
toleration, religious minorities 68–69
tradition, value of 122
two-pronged theory 114–115

ultra vires 61, 62
universal normative theory of minimal secularism 48–49

Vallier, Kevin 11, 34n6, 121
voluntary associations 98–99

Williams, Bernard 86